Just the Facts:
Life Science

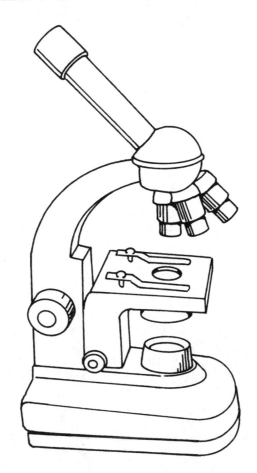

by Steve Rich

Carson-Dellosa Publishing Company, Inc.
Greensboro, North Carolina

CREDITS

EDITOR: Matthew Fisher

LAYOUT DESIGN: Lori Jackson

INSIDE ILLUSTRATIONS: Don O'Connor

COVER DESIGN: Peggy Jackson

PHOTO CREDITS: © PhotoDisc
© Corbis
© Brand X
© Digital Vision
© Liquidlibrary

Just the Facts: Life Science is dedicated to Glenn Russell Bilanin,
the primary person who reminds me of life beyond science.

Acknowledgements:

I am grateful for the inspiration of science educators and colleagues whom I have met through NSTA, the Presidential Award, GSTA, and GYSTC. I am also grateful for the inspiration of three generations: my precious grandmothers, Lucille Green Odom and Josephine Calloway Rich, for raising the incredible people who grew up to become my parents; my phenomenal mother and biggest fan, June Coleman Rich, a champion for all children—especially her own; and my science-teaching sister, Cathy Rich Robinson, whom I admire and love. Finally, I thank my son, Spencer Rich, for his willingness to share me with the world of science education and for exceeding my impossibly high expectations, while maintaining a unique sense of humor.

ISBN 978-1-59441-249-3

Just the Facts: Life Science

HUMAN BODY SYSTEMS

ADAPTATIONS

ECOSYSTEMS AND BIOMES

HUMANS AND THE ENVIRONMENT

Just the Facts: Life Science

There are millions of animals, plants, fungi, and microscopic organisms that live on Earth. Some are larger than trucks, while others are smaller than the heads of pins. Whatever sizes they may be, it is important to understand the importance of every living organism because each one plays an important role in the balance of Earth's natural systems. When one organism becomes extinct, it can create a ripple that will affect many other species.

How would the death of a fish population in a local pond affect the community? What great environmental purpose do the ants that gather food in the schoolyard serve? Biologists, ecologists, microbiologists, botanists, and other types of scientists have dedicated their lives to the study of how these organisms live, grow, and reproduce. Without basic scientific knowledge, they would not be able to make accurate observations, analyze data, or answer these and other life science questions.

In *Just the Facts: Life Science*, students will be exposed to basic, factual knowledge that will allow them to conduct inquiry investigations, much like the experiments that real-world scientists conduct every day. The worksheets and activities in this book will supplement your daily lessons, and some can be used as stepping-stones to full inquiry experiments that students can develop themselves.

How are organisms on Earth tied to each other? Armed with scientific facts and knowledge, scientists carry on the process of inquiry and discovery. Perhaps, one day, it will be one of your students who will reveal the truth.

A = Science as Inquiry
B = Physical Science
C = Life Science
D = Earth and Space Science

E = Science and Technology
F = Science in Personal and Social Perspectives
G = History and Nature of Science

ACTIVITY	A	B	C	D	E	F	G
Learning about Living Things (page 9)			X				
It's Alive! Word Search (page 10)			X				
What Does It Mean to Be Alive? (page 11)			X				
Scientists Who Study Life (page 12)			X			X	X
Learning about Cells (page 13)			X				
The Amazing Microscope (page 14)		X	X			X	X
What Is Inside a Cell? Word Search (page 15)			X				
What Is Inside a Cell? Crossword Puzzle (page 16)			X				
Label an Animal Cell (page 17)			X				
Label a Plant Cell (page 18)			X				
Comparing Plant and Animal Cells (page 19)			X				
Looking at Living Cells (page 20)	X		X				X
Can You Tell If It Is a Cell? (page 22)	X		X				
The Mystery of Cells (page 23)			X				
Creating a Cell Model (page 24)	X		X				
Why Do I Look Like Me? (page 25)			X			X	
The Cell Cycle Word Search (page 28)			X				
The Cell Cycle Crossword Puzzle (page 29)			X				
Cellular Division (page 30)			X				
Learning about Classification (page 31)			X				X
A System of Organization Word Search (page 32)			X				
A System of Organization Crossword Puzzle (page 33)			X				
Classifying Everyday Objects (page 34)	X		X				X
Let Me Count the Ways (page 35)	X		X				X
Remembering Taxonomy (page 36)			X				
How Scientists Classify Living Things (page 37)			X				
The Diversity of Life (page 38)			X				
Discovering New Rain Forest Species (page 39)	X		X				X
The Classified Ads (page 40)			X				
Comparing the Six Kingdoms (page 41)			X				
Learning about Simple Life Forms (page 42)			X				
Simple Life Forms Word Search (page 43)			X				
Simple Life Forms Crossword Puzzle (page 44)			X				
The Eubacteria Kingdom (page 45)			X				
Bacteria: Community Helper? (page 46)			X	X		X	
The Protist Kingdom (page 47)			X				
The Tale of Two Types of Protists (page 48)			X				
The Fungi Kingdom (page 49)			X				
You Be the Microbiologist (page 50)			X			X	X
Lichens, Mosses, and Algae (page 51)	X		X				
Life as a One-Celled Organism (page 53)			X				
How Well Do Household Cleaners Work? (page 54)	X		X			X	
Learning about the Plant Kingdom (page 55)			X				
A Kingdom of Plants Word Search (page 56)			X				
A Kingdom of Plants Crossword Puzzle (page 57)			X				
Parts of Vascular Plants (page 58)			X	X			
Comparing Plants (page 59)			X				
Getting the Seeds Out (page 60)			X				
What Is Inside a Seed? (page 61)			X				
When Seeds Fly (page 62)	X		X				

ACTIVITY	A	B	C	D	E	F	G
Growing Up, Growing Down (page 64)	X	X	X				
You Be the Botanist (page 65)			X			X	X
Year After Year (page 66)			X				
Plant Reproduction (page 67)			X				
Graphing Plant Growth (page 68)	X		X				
Learning about the Animal Kingdom (page 70)			X				
The Diversity of Animals Word Search (page 71)			X				
So Many Different Animals (page 72)			X				
Organization of Organisms (page 73)			X				
Observing Animal Objects (page 74)	X		X				
Life Cycle of a Frog (page 76)			X				
Life Cycle of a Butterfly (page 77)			X				
Vertebrate Animals (page 78)			X				
Invertebrate Animals (page 79)			X				
What Animals Need to Survive (page 81)			X			X	
You Be the Zoologist (page 82)			X			X	X
Amazing Animal Facts (page 83)			X				
Snakes in the Desert (page 84)	X		X	X			
Learning about the Human Body (page 85)			X				
Human Body Organs and Systems Word Search (page 86)			X				
Organ Systems of the Human Body (page 87)			X				
Name That Body System (page 88)			X				
Human Organs and Organ Systems (page 89)			X				
How Does Exercise Affect Your Heart Rate? (page 90)	X		X			X	
Amazing Human Body Math Facts (page 91)	X		X				
Digestion Math (page 92)			X				
A Day in the Life of a Cell (page 93)			X				
Learning about Adaptations (page 94)			X				
Changes Over Time Word Search (page 95)			X				
Changes Over Time Crossword Puzzle (page 96)			X				
Name the Animal Adaptation (page 97)			X				
More Than One Way to Hide (page 98)			X				
Plant Adaptations (page 99)			X				
Bird Adaptations (page 100)	X		X				
Creating New Adaptations (page 101)	X		X				
Organisms in Danger Word Search (page 102)			X				
Organisms in Danger Crossword Puzzle (page 103)			X				
Learning about Ecosystems (page 104)			X			X	
Pieces of the Ecosystem Puzzle Word Search (page 105)			X			X	
Pieces of the Ecosystem Puzzle Crossword Puzzle (page 106)			X			X	
The Chains of Life Word Search (page 107)			X			X	
The Chains of Life Crossword Puzzle (page 108)			X			X	
The Pyramid of Life (page 109)			X			X	
Biome Characteristics Word Search (page 110)			X				
Biome Characteristics Crossword Puzzle (page 111)			X				
What Is Each Biome Like? (page 112)			X				
Where Are the World's Biomes? (page 113)			X	X			
You Be the Ecologist (page 114)			X			X	X
Biomes Throughout the Year (page 115)	X		X				
Learning about Environmental Issues (page 116)			X	X		X	
Environmental Issues Word Search (page 117)			X	X		X	
Environmental Issues Crossword Puzzle (page 118)			X	X		X	
Pollution Solution (page 119)			X			X	
Ways You Can Help the Environment (page 120)			X			X	
Reduce, Reuse, and Recycle (page 121)			X	X		X	

INTRODUCTION

Show What You Know!

KWL CHART

DIRECTIONS: Before you begin learning about this topic, complete the first three sections of the **KWL** chart below. Under **K**, list what you already know about the topic. Under **W**, list what you would like to find out about the topic. Once you have studied the topic, come back to the chart and list what you learned under **L**.

TOPIC: _____

K What I Know	W What I Want to Know	L What I Have Learned

Learning about Living Things

DIRECTIONS: Context clues help us learn new words when we read. Use the words, phrases, and sentences around new words to determine their meanings. Look at the words in the chart and fill in the column "What I Think It Means." Read the passage and look for context clues to help determine the meanings of the words. Then, fill in the last column, "What It Means in Context." If your answer in the first column was completely correct, use the second column to add something to the word's meaning beyond your original ideas.

Word	What I Think It Means	What It Means in Context
alive		
cells		
develop		
respond		
reproduce		

What does it mean to be **alive**? What are some of the differences between a bird and a rock? What is the same about a tree and a mouse? Living things come in all shapes, sizes, and colors. You can easily see some living things, such as birds, trees, and people. Other living things, such as mold and bacteria, are too small to see without a microscope. All living things have several things in common. For example, they are all made of small units called cells. Some are made of only one cell, while others are made of millions of **cells**. The cells of living things need energy to work, grow, and repair themselves. All living things also need to create new cells as they grow and **develop** throughout their lives. Nonliving things, such as rocks and trucks, do not grow or develop.

If you jump out from behind a curtain to scare a friend, she might scream in response! Living things **respond**, or react, to their surroundings. A plant in a sunny window will grow toward the sunlight. A squirrel that sees a predator will respond by hiding in a tree. Nonliving things, such as telephones, do not respond to their environment.

All living things **reproduce**, or make other organisms that are similar to themselves. Trees make seeds that grow into new trees. Some lizards lay eggs that develop into young lizards. Some single-celled organisms split into two parts to make two new cells.

It's Alive!

DIRECTIONS: Find the life-science vocabulary words in the word search below. Words can be found down, across, and diagonally. Then, on a separate piece of paper, write sentences for five of the words.

WORD BANK

organism	stimulus	heterotroph	plants
unicellular	response	water	fungi
multicellular	reproduce	homeostasis	bacteria
develop	autotroph	animals	protists

```
F  Z  F  L  Y  K  C  P  E  W  L  A  N  I  M  A  L  S  N  Y
C  A  O  U  R  I  O  D  S  N  M  G  H  S  G  P  D  S  U  V
D  R  R  F  Y  V  S  S  L  B  P  P  O  P  K  H  M  U  W  Z
D  P  G  X  A  B  U  U  F  O  M  U  G  U  I  M  C  A  A  O
A  L  A  R  I  A  J  B  L  S  F  P  X  H  K  M  X  X  T  M
H  A  N  Z  T  C  G  E  R  F  Y  R  G  E  M  A  N  R  E  R
W  N  I  V  F  T  V  E  H  D  M  Y  C  T  U  U  S  E  R  L
D  T  S  O  O  E  D  Z  D  Z  S  M  T  E  L  T  N  S  P  I
M  S  M  S  D  R  Y  U  E  H  P  Y  K  R  T  O  P  P  B  J
T  U  B  C  U  I  Z  H  D  E  D  Q  O  O  I  T  P  O  K  U
E  N  A  F  P  A  N  D  B  H  Z  Z  N  T  C  R  F  N  T  M
N  I  O  H  U  R  P  S  J  G  V  I  G  R  E  O  D  S  B  F
J  C  F  Q  Z  T  O  G  T  A  D  V  Z  O  L  P  R  E  S  O
E  E  U  A  C  E  P  T  E  I  Y  X  S  P  L  H  X  G  I  C
Y  L  N  W  F  V  V  A  I  D  M  T  R  H  U  D  G  D  A  N
R  L  G  N  R  D  K  Z  T  S  L  U  E  W  L  E  Q  M  U  L
L  U  I  S  E  V  Z  N  W  K  T  G  L  B  A  N  G  Z  M  A
E  L  J  P  J  W  G  V  A  O  L  S  B  U  R  Y  M  S  S  Y
Y  A  U  Q  Y  R  E  P  R  O  D  U  C  E  S  O  X  P  U  V
W  R  P  H  Y  B  H  O  M  E  O  S  T  A  S  I  S  H  M  K
```

Name: _____ Date: _____

What Does It Mean to Be Alive?

MYSTERY WORD

DIRECTIONS: Fill in the blanks to match the words to the definitions below. Circle the designated letter or letters in each answer. Then, unscramble the circled letters to reveal the mystery word.

WORD BANK

| response | multicellular | stimulus | reproduce | organism |
| heterotroph | develop | unicellular | autotroph | homeostasis |

1. _____ a living thing (fifth letter)

2. _____ an organism that is made of only one cell (second letter)

3. _____ an organism that is made of many cells (fourth letter)

4. _____ an organism that makes its own food (first letter)

5. _____ how an organism reacts to a change in its environment (fourth letter)

6. _____ how an organism grows and changes throughout its life (second and sixth letters)

7. _____ how an organism creates new organisms that are similar to itself (seventh letter)

8. _____ an organism that cannot make its own food and eats plants or animals (sixth letter)

9. _____ how an organism maintains its internal body conditions, such as temperature and amount of water and nutrients (eleventh letter)

10. _____ a change in an environment that causes an organism to respond (first letter)

MYSTERY WORD

People once believed that living things might come from nonliving things.

This is called __ __ __ __ __ __ __ __ __ __ __ generation.

Name: _____   Date: _____

Scientists Who Study Life

No scientist could know everything about all of the living organisms on Earth—there are too many of them. Scientists who are interested in studying living organisms and ecosystems specialize in one specific area of study, such as animals or food chains. These scientists go to school for many years to become experts in their fields. They also write reports that often are published in scientific journals. What kind of life scientist would you like to be?

DIRECTIONS: Use the words in the word bank to match the scientists to the descriptions of what they study.

WORD BANK

zoologists	paleontologists	agronomists
marine biologists	botanists	entomologists
cell biologists	biologists	ecologists
anthropologists	geneticists	microbiologists

1. plant life _____

2. living and nonliving things in ecosystems _____

3. organisms that live in the ocean _____

4. growth and reproduction of cells _____

5. microscopic forms of life _____

6. relationship of organisms through DNA _____

7. farms, crops, and soil _____

8. classification and study of animals _____

9. all forms of living organisms _____

10. insects _____

11. fossils and life forms of the past _____

12. past and present-day human beings _____

Learning about Cells

DIRECTIONS: Context clues help us learn new words when we read. Use the words, phrases, and sentences around new words to determine their meanings. Look at the words in the chart and fill in the column "What I Think It Means." Read the passage and look for context clues to help determine the meanings of the words. Then, fill in the last column, "What It Means in Context." If your answer in the first column was completely correct, use the second column to add something to the word's meaning beyond your original ideas.

Word	What I Think It Means	What It Means in Context
unicellular		
multicellular		
microscope		
organelles		
nucleus		
function		

What are the most basic units of all living things? If you said, "Cells," you are right. If you look at the wall of your school, you may notice that it is made up of thousands of bricks. Just as bricks make up the parts of the wall, cells make up the parts of your body. All living plants and animals are composed of cells. Some plants and animals are **unicellular**, or have one cell, while others are **multicellular**, or have many cells.

Since cells are very small, you cannot see them with an unaided eye. You need to use a tool called a **microscope** to see cells. Microscopes make tiny objects look larger. Some microscopes can help you see groups of cells, and other microscopes are so powerful that they can help you see the tiny parts that make up the cells. Inside cells, there are **organelles**, structures that help the cell **function**. One organelle, called the **nucleus**, controls all of the cell's functions, including reproduction. Another organelle, called the mitochondria, produces energy that helps the cell function. All of the cell's organelles are important. They make sure that all of the cells in your body work properly.

CELLS

The Amazing Microscope

DIAGRAM LABELING

In 1663, an English scientist named **Robert Hooke** placed a piece of cork under a series of lenses. He called the things that he saw through the lens **cells**, because they looked like tiny, rectangular rooms. A scientist from Denmark named **Anton van Leeuwenhoek** also built his own microscope. When he looked at a sample of pond water through his microscope, he saw tiny organisms swimming in the water. Microscopes have come a long way since the days of those scientists. Scientists now have powerful microscopes that can help them see things that are extremely small. It is important for scientists to know the parts of a microscope and how to use one to do their work.

DIRECTIONS: Use the words in the word bank to label the diagram of the microscope below.

WORD BANK

fine focus knob	base	stage	nosepiece
arm	light source	coarse focus knob	body tube
objectives	diaphragm	stage clips	ocular (eyepiece)

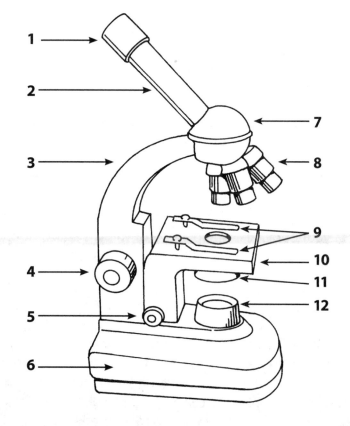

1. _____
2. _____
3. _____
4. _____
5. _____
6. _____
7. _____
8. _____
9. _____
10. _____
11. _____
12. _____

CELLS

What Is Inside a Cell?

WORD SEARCH

DIRECTIONS: Find the organelle vocabulary words in the word search below. Words can be found down, across, and diagonally. Then, on a separate piece of paper, write sentences for five of the words.

WORD BANK

cell membrane	DNA	ribosome
cytoplasm	Golgi bodies	vacuole
cell wall	nucleus	mitochondria
chloroplast	nucleolus	endoplasmic reticulum
chromosome	organelle	lysosome

```
F  R  I  B  O  S  O  M  E  J  L  X  M  F  J  E  Z  S  E  R
E  N  T  U  W  E  J  Z  N  L  K  S  K  I  L  B  U  Z  N  N
C  Q  M  L  W  R  C  K  A  P  A  Z  N  L  R  C  K  M  D  E
G  H  N  N  V  Q  G  W  A  L  D  D  E  F  Z  E  M  Y  O  N
C  O  J  M  X  K  L  I  P  H  O  N  C  R  X  B  I  C  P  U
E  S  L  O  C  L  J  O  Q  J  A  Q  R  L  F  M  T  H  L  C
L  G  D  G  E  V  T  Z  N  G  T  W  X  Y  Z  G  O  L  A  L
L  N  O  C  I  Y  G  T  R  Z  O  P  O  F  L  H  C  O  S  E
M  P  V  N  C  B  U  O  S  L  R  S  T  G  K  S  H  R  M  U
E  S  F  A  Q  F  O  E  I  L  Y  N  W  K  A  T  O  O  I  S
M  C  T  D  C  N  K  D  P  U  B  S  O  M  H  H  N  P  C  F
B  H  R  I  R  U  W  R  I  C  V  Z  O  I  E  A  D  L  R  L
R  R  B  E  C  C  O  A  O  E  Z  J  Z  S  N  H  R  A  E  G
A  O  E  F  O  L  K  L  U  E  S  E  V  D  O  I  I  S  T  L
N  M  N  G  E  E  K  W  E  N  F  T  C  S  K  M  A  T  I  T
E  O  W  Z  K  O  Z  G  O  I  N  N  O  V  F  D  E  F  C  U
J  S  U  Z  V  L  C  H  E  O  R  Q  P  H  Y  L  L  I  U  N
A  O  I  X  Y  U  W  H  H  U  L  S  J  L  Z  H  C  S  L  H
T  M  H  Z  R  S  F  F  T  U  Y  E  O  F  O  J  O  R  U  D
V  E  C  O  I  S  N  Q  Z  D  J  D  R  Y  X  R  B  N  M  M
```

Name: _____   Date: _____

What Is Inside a Cell?

DIRECTIONS: Complete the crossword puzzle.

ACROSS

2. package materials from the endoplasmic reticulum and send them to other parts of the cell

4. breaks down food and old cell parts

7. a stiff layer of nonliving material that surrounds a plant cell

8. jellylike material found within the cell membrane

10. found in plant cells; captures the sun's energy to make food

12. genetic materials that carry information about the organism

13. moves materials throughout the cell

DOWN

1. produce proteins for the cell

3. a tiny structure inside a cell

5. controls all of the cell's activities

6. produce most of the cell's energy

7. controls substances that enter and leave the cell

9. creates ribosomes; found inside the nucleus

11. stores water and waste inside the cell

CELLS

Label an Animal Cell

DIAGRAM LABELING

DIRECTIONS: Use the words in the word bank to label the parts of the animal cell.

WORD BANK

nucleus	vacuole	Golgi body
chromosomes	mitochondrion	lysosome
cell membrane	endoplasmic reticulum	ribosome
cytoplasm	nucleolus	

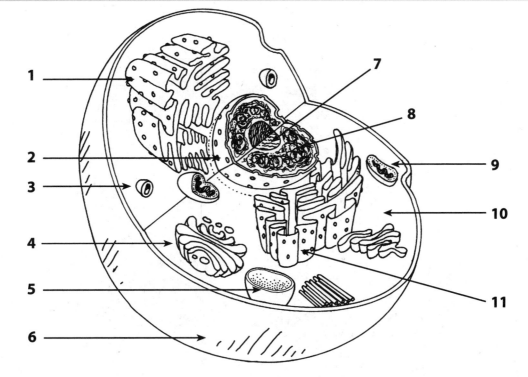

1. _____
2. _____
3. _____
4. _____
5. _____
6. _____

7. _____
8. _____
9. _____
10. _____
11. _____

CELLS

Label a Plant Cell

DIAGRAM LABELING

DIRECTIONS: Use the words in the word bank to label the parts of the plant cell.

WORD BANK

nucleus	cytoplasm	nucleolus
chromosomes	vacuole	endoplasmic reticulum
cell wall	chloroplast	
cell membrane	mitochondrion	

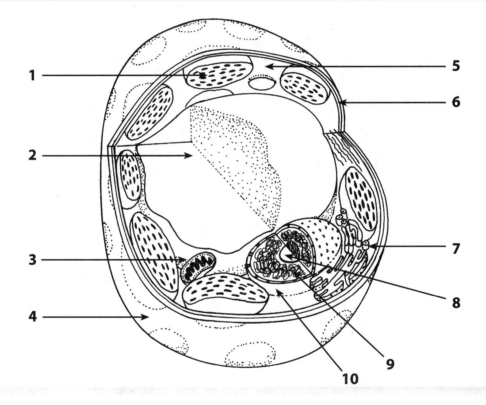

1. _____   6. _____

2. _____   7. _____

3. _____   8. _____

4. _____   9. _____

5. _____   10. _____

Name: _____ Date: _____

Comparing Plant and Animal Cells

FILL IN THE BLANKS

DIRECTIONS: How are animal cells and plant cells alike? How are they different? For each cell characteristic below, write *plant*, *animal*, or *both* in the blank.

1. _____ These cells have cell membranes.

2. _____ Chloroplasts are used by these cells for photosynthesis.

3. _____ These cells use mitosis to divide into two daughter cells.

4. _____ These cells are filled with a jellylike fluid called cytoplasm.

5. _____ Each of these cells has one or more large vacuoles.

6. _____ Instead of a few large vacuoles, these cells have several small vacuoles.

7. _____ These cells have cell walls.

8. _____ Each of these cells has a nucleus that controls all of the cell's functions.

9. _____ These cells have irregular shapes.

10. _____ These cells use lysosomes to break down food and old cell parts.

11. _____ These cells have mitochondria that help create energy for the cells.

12. _____ The cell wall usually gives each of these cells a rectangular shape.

13. Name three types of organisms that are made of plant cells. _____

_____

_____

14. Name three types of organisms that are made of animal cells. _____

_____

_____

15. On a separate piece of paper, organize the facts from this page into a paragraph that describes the similarities and differences between plant and animal cells.

CELLS

Looking at Living Cells

INQUIRY INVESTIGATION

In this inquiry investigation, you will reproduce the work of the Dutch scientist **Anton van Leeuwenhoek** by investigating a sample of pond water. What does a **unicellular** organism look like? How does it move? You will also be observing the cells of an **Elodea leaf**, a common freshwater plant that you can buy at a pet supply store or an aquarium store.

MATERIALS

sample of pond water	microscope	regular slide	eyedropper
Elodea leaf	well slide	cover slips	tap water

PROCEDURE:

1. Use the eyedropper to place one drop of pond water onto the well slide. Cover the pond water sample with the cover slip.

2. Place the slide on the microscope stage. Turn on the microscope and observe the sample on the microscope's lowest magnification.

3. Look for any objects that are moving or that resemble cells. When you find a unicellular organism, increase the magnification of the microscope.

4. Write your observations and sketch the cell on the chart on page 21. Label any organelles that you see. If you find more than one organism, draw and describe it on the second chart provided. Use a science book or the Internet to find the name of the organism that you found.

5. Place an Elodea leaf on a regular slide. Add one drop of tap water and cover the leaf with a cover slip. Place the slide on the microscope stage.

6. Observe the Elodea leaf on the microscope's lowest magnification. When you have focused it, increase the magnification.

7. Write your observations and sketch a picture of the Elodea leaf on the chart on page 21. Label any plant organelles that you see.

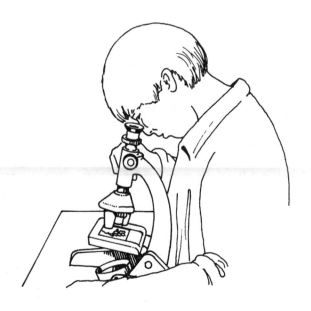

Unicellular Pond Organism 1

Observations

_____
_____
_____
_____
_____
_____
_____
_____

Unicellular Pond Organism 2

Observations

_____
_____
_____
_____
_____
_____
_____
_____
_____
_____

Elodea Leaf

Observations

_____
_____
_____
_____
_____
_____
_____
_____
_____

Can You Tell If It Is a Cell?

DIRECTIONS: Scientists use **data tables** to gather data and communicate the results of their experiments. The table below shows the data that was collected by a scientist who observed objects on five separate microscope slides. He was looking for plant or animal cells. Use the data to answer the questions.

Slide	Nucleus?	Cell Wall?	Chloroplasts?	Uni- or Multicellular?
1	yes	?	yes	multi
2	yes	no	no	multi
3	no	?	no	multi
4	yes	no	no	uni
5	?	yes	no	uni

1. If the observations that were made by the scientist are correct, how many of the slides definitely contain a cell? What percentage of the slides is this?

   _____

2. Although the scientist could not find a cell wall in slide one, what other data would make him believe that it is a plant cell?

   _____

   _____

3. Slide 5 appears to have a cell wall. Can the scientist be sure that it is a plant cell?

   _____

   _____

4. One of the slides contains a human blood cell. Explain how you can narrow your choices down to two of the slides.

   _____

   _____

5. The scientist suspects that slide 5 is a cell but could not observe a nucleus. How could he prove that it is a cell?

   _____

   _____

Name: _____   Date: _____

The Mystery of Cells

M Y S T E R Y   W O R D S

DIRECTIONS: Fill in the blanks to complete the sentences below. Circle the designated letter or letters in each answer. Then, unscramble the circled letters to reveal the mystery words.

WORD BANK

identical	nucleus	endoplasmic reticulum
chlorophyll	cells	organelles
chromosomes	interphase	replace

1. _____ New cells can grow and _____ damaged or dead cells. (sixth letter)

2. _____ In the first stage of cell reproduction, the _____ disappears. (fourth letter)

3. _____ Before mitosis begins, the cell's _____, such as chloroplast and mitochondria, make copies of themselves. (seventh letter)

4. _____ The period of time when a cell grows and copies its DNA is called _____. (fourth letter)

5. _____ _____ are the basic units of structure in all living organisms. (first letter)

6. _____ After mitosis, two _____ daughter cells are created. (ninth letter)

7. _____ After mitosis, each daughter cell should have a complete set of _____. (first letter)

8. _____ Plant cells use _____ to capture sunlight. (ninth letter)

9. _____ The _____ transports materials and proteins throughout the cell. (first letter)

MYSTERY WORDS

Most cells go through a process of growth and reproduction called the

__ __ __ __   __ __ __ __ __ __ .

CELLS

Creating a Cell Model

CREATING A MODEL

Cells are so small that we need microscopes to see them. Scientists often make **models** to observe objects that are too small to see.

DIRECTIONS: Work with a partner to create a model of a plant or animal cell using common materials. In the chart below, pick a type of material to represent each organelle. Use the materials listed below to create your model. Then, on a separate piece of paper, write a paragraph that describes why you chose each type of material to represent each organelle. Does the organelle look like the material? Do they have the same texture or shape?

MATERIALS

buttons	beads	different shapes, sizes, and colors of pasta
small plastic bags	chenille craft sticks	
vegetable oil	plastic cups and bowls	any additional teacher-approved materials
bottle caps	colorful yarn	

Organelle	Material Used in the Model
cell wall	
cell membrane	
cytoplasm	
nucleus	
ribosome	
chloroplast	
lysosome	
chromosomes	
Golgi body	
nucleolus	
vacuole	
mitochondrion	
endoplasmic reticulum	

CELLS

Why Do I Look Like Me?

INQUIRY INVESTIGATION

Look at yourself in the mirror. Does your nose look like your mother's or father's nose? Does your sister look like you? Your **genes** determine your physical characteristics. They decide the color of your hair, the size of your feet, the shape of your chin, and many other things. Your parents pass their genes on to you. You receive two genes for every trait—one from your mother and one from your father. Some genes are **dominant** (represented by uppercase letters). If you do not have any dominant genes for a characteristic, your genes are **recessive** (represented by lowercase letters) for that trait.

PROCEDURE: Read about each of the physical traits that are listed below. Write the correct response in each blank based on the physical traits that you have.

WIDOW'S PEAK: A dominant gene causes a widow's peak. If you have a widow's peak, you have a dominant gene for that trait. You need only one dominant gene for this characteristic, so your genes are **W–**. Since you cannot tell whether the second gene is dominant or recessive, leave it blank.

If you do not have a widow's peak, you have a **recessive** gene for that trait. This means that neither of your parents passed the dominant gene to you, and your genes are **ww**.

My genes are (dominant/recessive) for a widow's peak. _____

My genes are (W–/ww). _____

UNATTACHED EARLOBES: A dominant gene causes earlobes to be unattached at the bottoms. If your earlobes are unattached at the bottoms, you have a **dominant** gene for that trait. If your earlobes are completely attached to the sides of your head, you have a **recessive** gene for that trait.

My genes are (dominant/recessive) for unattached earlobes. _____

My genes are (E–/ee). _____

TONGUE ROLLING: A dominant gene allows you to stick out your tongue and roll it into a U shape. If you can roll your tongue into a U shape, you have a **dominant** gene for that trait. If you cannot roll your tongue into a U shape, you have a **recessive** gene for that trait.

My genes are (dominant/recessive) for tongue rolling. _____

My genes are (T–/tt). _____

BENT LITTLE FINGER: A dominant gene causes your little finger to bend inward toward your ring finger. If your little finger bends inward, you have a **dominant** gene for that trait. If your little finger does not bend inward toward your ring finger, you have a **recessive** gene for that trait.

My genes are (dominant/recessive) for a bent little finger. _____

My genes are (B–/bb). _____

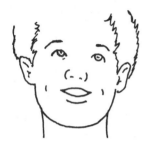

FACIAL DIMPLES: A dominant gene causes you to have facial dimples at the corners of your mouth when you smile. If you have dimples when you smile, you have a **dominant** gene for that trait. If you do not have dimples when you smile, you have a **recessive** gene for that trait.

My genes are (dominant/recessive) for having dimples. _____

My genes are (D–/dd). _____

STRAIGHT THUMB: A dominant gene causes your thumb to be straight when you give a thumbs-up. If your thumb is straight, you have a **dominant** gene for that trait. If your thumb is curved when you give a thumbs-up, you have a **recessive** gene for that trait.

My genes are (dominant/recessive) for a straight thumb. _____

My genes are (S–/ss). _____

Based on the characteristics that you exhibit, predict which characteristics your parents have. Remember, in order for you have dominant genes for a trait, you need only one parent to have passed that gene on to you. If your genes are recessive, neither parent passed that gene to you.

Predictions

Characteristic	Mom		Dad	
	Yes	No	Yes	No
Widow's Peak				
Unattached Earlobes				
Tongue Rolling				
Bent Little Finger				
Facial Dimples				
Straight Thumb				

After you make your predictions on page 26, check them by asking your parents which physical traits they have from pages 25 and 26. Then, complete the observations chart and questions below.

Observations of Parents

Characteristic	Mom		Dad	
	Yes	No	Yes	No
Widow's Peak				
Unattached Earlobes				
Tongue Rolling				
Bent Little Finger				
Facial Dimples				
Straight Thumb				

1. Which of your parents' traits did you predict correctly?

   _____

   _____

   _____

2. Which of your parents' traits were more difficult to predict? Why?

   _____

   _____

   _____

3. Is it possible for you to display recessive traits when one parent has a dominant trait? If so, how?

   _____

   _____

   _____

   _____

The Cell Cycle

WORD SEARCH

DIRECTIONS: Find the cell-cycle vocabulary words in the word search below. Words can be found down, across, and diagonally. Then, on a separate piece of paper, write sentences for five of the words.

WORD BANK

chromosomes	chromatid	cytokinesis	metaphase
DNA	interphase	centromere	prophase
nucleus	cytoplasm	mitosis	telophase
cell membrane	daughter cells	cell cycle	anaphase

```
G T K Z Y W M G D K X B H Q M M P V W E
D D S V A V Y Q L D S B V B S U L N S C
A P C Y T O K I N E S I S A T D D I L H
Z C R D N X W F B Q T Q L H I G S Y M R
K E L F P R P C D F Q P K F N O X C C O
Y L I M R T H M L Y O J J L T U E E R M
N L A C O L E F L T L Y V I E H P L G O
L C C H P Z F L Y K B N M P R U J L U S
U Y T R H V W C O H O U Z T P D L M A O
V C J O A F K I S P D H G I H X H E N M
L L A M S M E T A P H A S E A R J M A E
V E M A E C C R O U U A D E S G X B P S
I X P T M Q L A C Y S D S N E G G R H M
W Q B I Q F X R O H W X N E A G Q A A M
Q I G D P U P Q Q T N U C L E U S N S Y
G C E N T R O M E R E R Y N M C A E E U
D D A U G H T E R C E L L S A S C R B I
```

The Cell Cycle

CROSSWORD PUZZLE

DIRECTIONS: Complete the crossword puzzle.

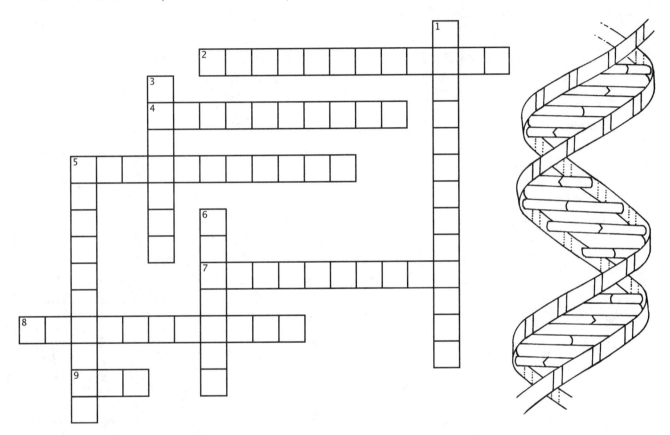

ACROSS

2. structure that controls substances that enter and leave the cell

4. phase when the cell grows, copies its DNA, and gets ready to divide

5. contain DNA, which holds the genetic information of the cell

7. organelle that forms spindle fibers that split and pull chromosomes to opposite ends of the cell

8. final phase of mitosis; the cytoplasm divides, and the cell's organelles are placed in two new cells.

9. genetic material that carries information about an organism

DOWN

1. two cells that are created after mitosis

3. all cells go through this process of growing and dividing

5. each chromosome is made of these two identical parts

6. control center of cell; directs all cell functions; contains DNA

Cellular Division

M A T H   S K I L L S

DIRECTIONS: Answer the following math problems. Use the space below each problem or a separate piece of paper to show your work.

1. The red bone marrow in a human's bones produces about 2,000,000 red blood cells every second. How many red blood cells are produced in 1 minute?

Answer: _____

2. If a young plant has 128 cells, how many times has it gone through the process of mitosis?

Answer: _____

3. A human red blood cell lives for about 120 days. How many hours does it live? Minutes? Seconds?

Answers: _____

_____

_____

4. A typical human-body cell has 46 chromosomes. If half of them come from each parent, how many chromosomes does each parent contribute?

Answer: _____

5. Complete the chart below to show the number of cells that are produced by a single cell that goes through mitosis.

Division Number	Total Number of Cells
1	2
2	
3	
4	
5	
6	
7	
8	
9	
10	

Name: _____ Date: _____

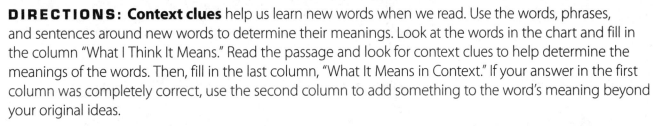

Learning about Classification

CONTEXT CLUES

DIRECTIONS: Context clues help us learn new words when we read. Use the words, phrases, and sentences around new words to determine their meanings. Look at the words in the chart and fill in the column "What I Think It Means." Read the passage and look for context clues to help determine the meanings of the words. Then, fill in the last column, "What It Means in Context." If your answer in the first column was completely correct, use the second column to add something to the word's meaning beyond your original ideas.

Word	What I Think It Means	What It Means in Context
organisms		
kingdoms		
characteristics		
species		
vertebrate		

Scientists refer to all living things in the world, as **organisms**. An organism can be grouped into one of six kingdoms. The six **kingdoms** include plants, animals, protists, eubacteria, archaebacteria, and fungi. These are the largest groups in which organisms can be placed for identification. After kingdoms, organisms can be further divided by various **characteristics** that they share. When thinking about species, think about the word *specific*. **Species** is the smallest group into which organisms can be divided and is the one that is the most precise.

Scientists use Latin scientific names so that everyone around the world can use the same name. For example, scientists in France and Spain have different names in their languages for a killer whale. By using the Latin scientific name *Orcinus orca*, each scientist knows what animal the other is talking about. Scientists use the specific details and characteristics of organisms to put them in similar groups. For example, the characteristic of having a backbone, being a **vertebrate**, puts the killer whale into the phylum Chordata. Giving birth to live babies instead of laying eggs is one of the characteristics that put killer whales into the class Mammalia.

CLASSIFICATION

A System of Organization

WORD SEARCH

DIRECTIONS: Find the classification vocabulary words in the word search below. Words can be found down, across, and diagonally. Then, on a separate piece of paper, write sentences for five of the words.

WORD BANK

class	scientific name	fungi	Carolus Linnaeus
family	species	archaebacteria	multicellular
genus	structures	eubacteria	unicellular
kingdom	classification	protist	eukaryotes
order	animal	vertebrates	prokaryotes
phylum	plant	invertebrates	taxonomy

```
K  O  H  G  W  F  K  R  Q  P  B  S  I  D  U  N  C  F  E  D
I  Q  Y  M  F  C  A  H  E  C  Z  C  O  V  J  X  G  Z  I  C
N  S  F  E  T  B  I  M  X  H  T  I  X  P  L  Q  E  E  U  A
G  U  U  K  T  S  G  A  I  A  B  E  I  U  K  N  N  C  P  R
D  Z  N  O  R  D  E  R  W  L  E  N  N  U  M  N  U  L  L  O
O  Y  G  P  X  Q  G  B  G  H  Y  T  V  N  U  D  S  A  A  L
M  P  I  J  R  Y  Q  L  Q  R  P  I  E  I  L  R  E  S  N  U
W  U  R  V  V  O  P  B  Z  D  G  F  R  C  T  I  U  S  T  S
S  U  I  O  J  X  T  H  C  W  H  I  T  E  I  P  K  I  B  L
S  S  K  A  K  T  O  I  Y  T  N  C  E  L  C  O  A  F  P  I
T  P  T  E  K  A  V  R  S  L  C  N  B  L  E  Y  R  I  C  N
R  E  A  U  S  T  R  U  R  T  U  A  R  U  L  O  Y  C  F  N
U  C  X  B  E  X  C  Y  L  G  H  M  A  L  L  A  O  A  M  A
C  I  O  A  I  U  L  G  O  T  R  E  T  A  U  P  T  T  M  E
T  E  N  C  K  I  A  P  B  T  N  X  E  R  L  M  E  I  Z  U
U  S  O  T  Y  M  S  O  Q  N  E  A  S  J  A  I  S  O  J  S
R  Y  M  E  G  W  S  U  U  C  E  S  Y  M  R  B  A  N  Z  R
E  I  Y  R  C  U  A  R  C  H  A  E  B  A  C  T  E  R  I  A
S  V  F  I  N  N  M  A  N  I  M  A  L  M  M  M  P  L  G  B
C  Z  X  A  V  E  R  T  E  B  R  A  T  E  S  K  Z  N  A  D
```

A System of Organization

CROSSWORD PUZZLE

DIRECTIONS: Complete the crossword puzzle.

ACROSS

2. animals without backbones

3. kingdom of multicellular organisms that use photosynthesis to create their own food

9. most organisms in this kingdom are multicellular organisms that obtain food by breaking down decaying material

10. kingdom of unicellular organisms found in areas with extremely hot or acidic conditions

11. most organisms in this kingdom are unicellular, others form colonies or are multicellular; includes algae and slime molds

12. an organized system of classification

DOWN

1. animals with backbones

4. kingdom of multicellular organisms; includes mammals, reptiles, and amphibians

5. Swedish scientist who developed the system of taxonomy

6. cells with organized nuclei

7. cells without organized nuclei

8. unicellular organisms found everywhere on Earth; some are harmful, while others are helpful

Name: _____ Date: _____

Classifying Everyday Objects

DIRECTIONS: Classification is the process of grouping objects together based on their characteristics. You classify objects every day. In this activity, you will classify the objects in each word bank by placing them in the correct columns of the charts.

WORD BANK

pencil	checkbook	textbook	gym shorts	calculator
notebook	key ring	cell phone	deodorant	wallet
lipstick	tennis shoes	socks	paper	towel

Found in a Backpack	Found in a Gym Bag	Found in a Purse

For the second chart, decide what the column headings should be. Then, classify the list of animals.

WORD BANK

squirrel	frog	alligator	raven	goose
snake	monkey	bear	mosquito	trout
hawk	tortoise	whale	crab	owl

Name: _____   Date: _____

Let Me Count the Ways

INQUIRY INVESTIGATION

How many ways can you divide a group of 18 objects? What categories can you place them in? In this activity, you will work in a group of 3–4 students as you practice your classification skills.

MATERIALS

die	paper clips	rubber bands	pencils
various sizes, shapes, and colors of the following materials:	toothpicks	erasers	any additional teacher-approved materials
	twist ties	crayons	

PROCEDURE:

1. Your group will be given 18 varied items from the materials list above.

2. Each student should take a turn rolling the die.

3. Classify the items into the same amount of groups as the number that is rolled on the die. Write the category names on the chart below.

4. Pass the die to the next student. Each student should have five chances to roll the die and group the objects. You can play until no new ways to classify the objects can be found. The student who classifies the objects the most times is the winner.

	Name of Categories					
Number on Cube	1	2	3	4	5	6

Remembering Taxonomy

DIRECTIONS: How can you remember the order of the taxonomic system? The correct order of classification is **kingdom**, **phylum**, **class**, **order**, **family**, **genus**, and **species**. You can create a sentence, phrase, or poem to help you remember this system. An example sentence is given below. Try to come up with two of your own.

Example: **K**itchen **P**atrol **C**omes **O**n **F**riday, **G**reat **S**cott!

K _____   K _____

P _____   P _____

C _____   C _____

O _____   O _____

F _____   F _____

G _____   G _____

S _____   S _____

Share your phrases with two of your classmates. Write their original phrases below.

K _____   K _____

P _____   P _____

C _____   C _____

O _____   O _____

F _____   F _____

G _____   G _____

S _____   S _____

Name: _____ Date: _____

How Scientists Classify Living Things

FILL IN THE BLANKS

DIRECTIONS: Use the words in the word bank to fill in the blanks for the sentences below.

WORD BANK

amphibians	eubacteria	classification	kingdoms	plant
fungi	archaebacteria	invertebrates	protist	animal
mammals	species	nonvascular	vertebrates	

1. _____ When scientists group objects together according to their characteristics, this process is called _____.

2. _____ Each living creature is grouped into one of six _____.

3. _____ The _____ kingdom includes decomposers, such as mushrooms.

4. _____ Multicellular organisms that use sunlight to create food are grouped into the _____ kingdom.

5. _____ _____ are vertebrates that are warm-blooded, have hair, and give birth to live young.

6. _____ The _____ kingdom can be divided into two groups; those with backbones and those without.

7. _____ Organisms that have backbones are called _____.

8. _____ Organisms that do not have backbones are called _____.

9. _____ The smallest groups into which organisms can be classified are _____.

10. _____ Plants that do not have a system of tubes are called _____. These plants pass water and nutrients between their cells.

11. _____ One group of animal vertebrates called _____ start their lives in the water but move onto land as adults.

12. _____ These three kingdoms contain unicellular organisms.

_____

_____

CLASSIFICATION

The Diversity of Life

MATH SKILLS

DIRECTIONS: Answer the following math problems. Use the space below each problem or a separate piece of paper to show your work.

1. There are more species of insects than all other animals on Earth combined. Of the 1,500,000 species of insects, about 100,000 are found in North America. How many species of insects are found in other parts of the world?

   Answer: _____

2. The tropical rain forests have the greatest diversity of life of all places on land. If 4,000 different species of animals and plants can be found in a 25 square mile section of the rain forest, what is the average number of species per square mile?

   Answer: _____

3. The two main classifications of plants are vascular and nonvascular. Vascular plants, such as trees, absorb water through their roots and transport it up through tubes in their trunks and stems. The African Baobab tree can store 95,000 liters of water. If the tree needs to store that amount of water to last 12 months, how many liters of water does it use each month?

   Answer: _____

4. Spiders are classified in a different group than insects because spiders have 8 legs and insects have 6. If you have a collection of 11 spiders and 12 insects, how many total legs are there in the collection?

   Answer: _____

5. Use the list of animals below to answer the following questions:

snake	tiger	horse
turtle	zebra	raccoon
lizard	mouse	monkey

   a. What percentage of the animals are mammals?

   Answer: _____

   b. Write a fraction to show how many of the total animals are reptiles.

   Answer: _____

   c. What percentage of the animals are vertebrates?

   Answer: _____

Name: _____ Date: _____

Discovering New Rain Forest Species

DIRECTIONS: Imagine that you are a scientist living in a South American rain forest. You have gathered the following information about some unusual plants and animals that you have observed. Use the data chart to answer the questions below.

Kingdom	Looks Like a . . .	Characteristics	Number Seen
Plant	small fern	purple leaves	81
Plant	dogwood tree	yellow flowers	1
Animal	tiger	white fur	1
Animal	snail	very large	21
Animal	butterfly	no antennae	1

1. Which animal is most likely a new type of species? Why?

_____

_____

2. Which animals are most likely not new types of species? Why?

_____

_____

3. Which of the two plants may be a new species? Why?

_____

_____

4. How can you conclude that you observed a new species in this rain forest?

_____

_____

5. If the snail is not a new species, what are some reasons that it might be larger than the same species in another location?

_____

_____

_____

CLASSIFICATION

The Classified Ads

CREATIVE WRITING

DIRECTIONS: Imagine that you are the editor for the classified advertising section of your local newspaper. Write several advertisements to sell items to living things from the animal and plant kingdoms. What kinds of objects do plants or animals have that another plant or animal would want or need? Use the sample advertisements below to help you create your own original advertisements.

Animal Classified Advertisement

I am a medium-sized hermit who has outgrown his shell.

I am offering my old shell-home for a long-term lease. It is clean and has no cracks or leaks.

Please, serious saltwater inquiries only.
You can find me on the beach, under Pier 12.

Plant Classified Advertisement

We are a package of 20 sunflower seeds looking for a great location to grow.

We must have access to water, fertile soil, and bright, direct sunshine.

We are also interested in areas with plenty of birds and squirrels that can help transport our new seeds in the fall.

Animal Classified Advertisement

_____
_____
_____
_____
_____
_____
_____
_____

Plant Classified Advertisement

_____
_____
_____
_____
_____
_____
_____
_____

Comparing the Six Kingdoms

FILL IN THE CHART

DIRECTIONS: After you have learned about each of the six kingdoms, complete the chart below by identifying the kingdom in which each organism belongs. Write at least one characteristic that places the organism in its kingdom.

Name of Organism	Kingdom	Characteristic
1. paramecium		
2. oak tree		
3. mushroom		
4. sea urchin		
5. bacteria in a sink		
6. spider		
7. giant kelp		
8. amoeba		
9. yeast		
10. bee		
11. eagle		
12. sunflower		
13. mouse		
14. slime mold		
15. angelfish		
16. iguana		
17. sponge		
18. water mold		
19. bacteria in a hot spring		

Learning about Simple Life Forms

DIRECTIONS: Context clues help us learn new words when we read. Use the words, phrases, and sentences around new words to determine their meanings. Look at the words in the chart and fill in the column "What I Think It Means." Read the passage and look for context clues to help determine the meanings of the words. Then, fill in the last column, "What It Means in Context." If your answer in the first column was completely correct, use the second column to add something to the word's meaning beyond your original ideas.

Word	What I Think It Means	What It Means in Context
bacteria		
protist		
parasites		
fungi		
mold		

Even though simple life forms are small and not as complex as plants and animals, they still have distinguishing characteristics. **Bacteria** are single-celled organisms that do not have a nucleus. Some bacteria are capable of photosynthesis, using sunlight to produce food, while others absorb food from their surroundings. Sometimes, they are even **parasites**, living on and benefiting from plants or animals. Bacteria may live in extreme environments, such as hot springs, swamps, or the deep sea.

The **protist** kingdom is very diverse. Some organisms in this kingdom can be single-celled, while others are made of many cells. Some protists get their food from their environments, while others create it through photosynthesis. Some protists are parasites, which means they live in or on other organisms and can cause harm as they steal their nutrients. While they have many differences, one characteristic that protists share is that all of their cells have an organized nucleus.

Fungi are often multi-celled but can also be single-celled. Each cell of a fungus contains a nucleus. Fungi are not capable of photosynthesis, so they must absorb food from their surroundings. Humans eat some types of fungi, such as mushrooms. Many types of mushrooms are poisonous, so you should never eat a mushroom unless you know that it is safe. Another type of fungi, **mold**, can grow on food. You should never eat food that has mold on it.

Name: _____ Date: _____

Simple Life Forms

DIRECTIONS: Find the simple life forms vocabulary words in the word search below. Words can be found down, across, and diagonally. Then, on a separate piece of paper, write sentences for five of the words.

WORD BANK

lichen	slime mold	eukaryote	bacteria	heterotroph
giant kelp	algae	flagella	protists	hyphae
paramecium	nucleus	cytoplasm	photosynthesis	spores
mushroom	prokaryote	fungi	autotroph	

```
R  K  C  I  U  B  M  H  G  U  Z  K  O  G  L  O  C  D  M  E
L  Z  Y  J  C  A  N  H  A  P  A  R  A  M  E  C  I  U  M  I
Q  J  T  P  Y  F  Q  D  O  W  C  E  U  K  A  R  Y  O  T  E
T  Y  O  B  B  T  H  Z  L  W  T  P  Q  A  Y  H  G  A  R  Z
X  J  P  R  M  P  H  W  N  D  Q  H  Y  P  H  A  E  U  Z  A
R  O  L  F  J  X  H  E  R  N  U  C  L  E  U  S  P  T  Z  C
V  F  A  Z  H  W  H  O  L  B  A  C  T  E  R  I  A  O  B  Y
C  L  S  B  W  C  H  E  T  E  R  O  T  R  O  P  H  T  K  L
P  A  M  Y  I  A  Q  S  D  O  O  N  D  S  C  C  K  R  M  O
R  G  V  L  P  X  L  O  L  J  S  V  I  M  C  S  B  O  X  O
O  E  S  K  J  T  K  G  K  I  X  Y  D  M  T  O  O  P  H  X
K  L  T  G  M  R  T  G  A  Q  M  C  N  S  A  R  I  H  M  Z
A  L  A  T  I  J  I  I  O  E  U  E  I  T  H  A  B  B  S  P
R  A  V  S  O  G  Z  A  P  H  B  T  M  S  H  M  P  O  P  I
Y  Z  L  N  N  Q  O  N  B  U  O  L  U  O  B  E  D  Q  O  M
O  V  S  U  F  H  M  T  Q  R  S  M  C  A  L  M  S  E  R  D
T  G  F  K  W  M  V  K  P  J  D  Y  W  X  O  D  A  I  E  O
E  V  G  J  K  F  S  E  B  G  Z  M  L  E  C  D  W  R  S  N
Y  M  D  D  J  J  H  L  L  F  C  Q  D  R  V  M  P  B  Z  W
V  A  V  P  W  K  F  P  P  I  P  Z  G  N  O  G  Z  S  W  B
```

Simple Life Forms

CROSSWORD PUZZLE

DIRECTIONS: Complete the crossword puzzle.

ACROSS

5. an organism that is a combination of fungus and algae

9. the control center of cells; not found in bacteria

10. single-celled organisms that can be helpful or harmful; contain no nucleus; found everywhere on Earth

12. cell that does not have a nucleus

13. an organism that can create its own food through photosynthesis

DOWN

1. structures that absorb nutrients for fungi

2. organisms in this kingdom can be found in extremely hot, acidic, or salty locations

3. organism that eats another organism for food

4. type of protist that performs photosynthesis to make its own food

6. structures for fungi reproduction

7. cell that has a nucleus

8. structures that help bacteria move

11. organisms in this kingdom can be uni- or multi-celled; can be autotrophs or heterotrophs

Name: _____ Date: _____

The Eubacteria Kingdom

Bacteria are everywhere. There is nowhere on Earth, including on your skin, inside rocks, in the soil, and inside your stomach, that you would not find them. There are three basic shapes of bacteria—rod, spiral, and sphere. Bacteria can be both helpful and harmful to humans. They are helpful in the creation of foods, such as cheese and yogurt, but can also cause diseases, such as strep throat and food poisoning.

DIRECTIONS: Use the set of words in the first word bank to label the picture of the bacterium below. Then, use the second set of words to complete the following sentences.

WORD BANK

cell wall	cytoplasm	ribosomes
DNA	plasma membrane	flagellum

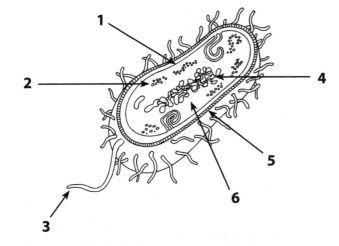

1. _____

2. _____

3. _____

4. _____

5. _____

6. _____

WORD BANK

disease	yogurt	spiral	prokaryotes
rod	sphere	flagella	

7. Bacteria can be helpful or can cause _____.

8. Bacteria lack nuclei, which means that they are _____.

9. Bacteria can be three different shapes: _____ , _____ , and _____.

10. The _____ help bacteria move by spinning like propellers.

11. Bacteria are useful in the creation of dairy products, such as _____.

SIMPLE LIFE FORMS

Bacteria: Community Helper?

MATCHING AND DRAWING

DIRECTIONS: Some types of bacteria are **beneficial**, or helpful to the plants and animals in an ecosystem. Match each use of bacteria with where the activity would take place. Then, in the boxes below, draw two ways that bacteria are beneficial.

1. _____ human stomach

2. _____ water treatment plant

3. _____ doctor's office

4. _____ oil spill in the ocean

5. _____ roots of a peanut plant

6. _____ food processing plant

7. _____ farmyard

8. _____ dairy processing plant

9. _____ home heating fuel

10. _____ landfills

a. is used in penicillin shots to cure infections

b. helps digest food

c. breaks down community sewage

d. produces nitrogen for animals and plants

e. breaks down harmful materials and pollutants

f. makes cheese, yogurt, and buttermilk

g. is added to cabbage to make sauerkraut

h. breaks down garbage

i. produces methane gas

j. breaks down animal waste

Name: _____ Date: _____

The Protist Kingdom

DIAGRAM LABELING

The **protist kingdom** includes a great diversity of organisms. Most protists, such as paramecium and amoeba, are unicellular, while others, such as giant kelp, are multicellular. Plantlike protists are **autotrophs**, and fungi- and animallike protists are **heterotrophs**. The organisms in the protist kingdom may be very different, but they do share some characteristics. All protists are **eukaryotes**, which means each of their cells has a nucleus. All protists can also be found in moist environments.

DIRECTIONS: Use the first set of words in the word bank to label the picture of the paramecium, an animallike protist. Then, use the second set of words to label the giant kelp, a plantlike protist.

WORD BANK

anal pore	micronucleus	oral groove
cilia	food vacuole	macronucleus
cytoplasm	cell membrane	

holdfast	blade	stipe	frond	gas bladder

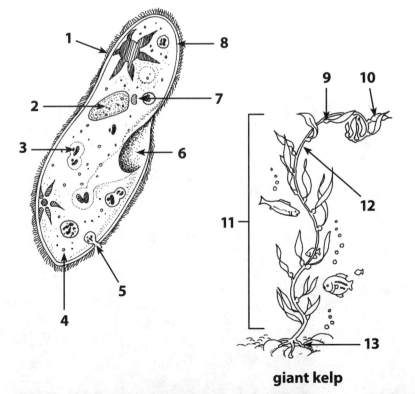

paramecium

giant kelp

1. _____
2. _____
3. _____
4. _____
5. _____
6. _____
7. _____
8. _____
9. _____
10. _____
11. _____
12. _____
13. _____

SIMPLE LIFE FORMS

The Tale of Two Types of Protists

MYSTERY WORDS

DIRECTIONS: Fill in the blanks to complete the sentences below. Circle the designated letter or letters in each answer. Then, unscramble the circled letters to reveal the mystery words.

WORD BANK

freshwater	blades	marine
anal pore	holdfast	cytoplasm
vacuole	gas bladders	giant kelp

1. _____ A paramecium's organelles are found in the _____, a jellylike fluid. (second and eighth letters)

2. _____ Paramecium can be found in many _____ environments. (third and eighth letters)

3. _____ When food is inside the paramecium, it is surrounded by a food _____. (fourth letter)

4. _____ A paramecium releases waste through a small opening called the _____. (first and sixth letters)

5. _____ Brown algae can be found in _____ environments. (first, fourth, and sixth letters)

6. _____ A _____ is used by the giant kelp to anchor itself to rocks. (second and eighth letters)

7. _____ Gas-filled sacs called _____ help the kelp float in water. (tenth letter)

8. _____ The _____ of the kelp are similar to leaves of trees. (sixth letter)

9. _____ The _____ is a multicellular, plantlike protist. (sixth letter)

MYSTERY WORDS

All protists are ___ ___ ___ ___ ___ ___ ___ ___ ___ ___ and live in

___ ___ ___ ___ ___ environments.

The Fungi Kingdom

Fungi are nature's decomposers. They can be unicellular or multicellular. They grow in moist, warm places and reproduce using spores. Some fungi, such as yeast and certain types of mushrooms, can be eaten and are helpful. Other types of fungi can cause serious diseases in crops. Fungi are **heterotrophs**, which means that they are organisms that cannot make their own food. There are four groups of fungi—sac, threadlike, club, and imperfect.

DIRECTIONS: Use the words in the word bank to label the fungus diagram. Then, match each word to its definition.

WORD BANK

hyphae	cap	gills	stalk	scales

1. _____
2. _____
3. _____
4. _____
5. _____

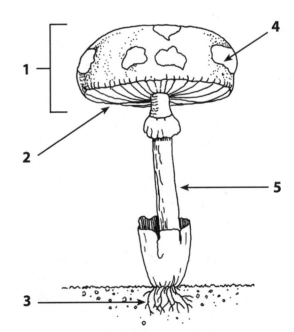

6. _____ the top part of the mushroom

7. _____ flat surfaces located on the underside of the cap, where spores are created

8. _____ rootlike filaments that anchor the mushroom in the soil

9. _____ the main support of the mushroom, which is topped by the cap

10. _____ rough patches of tissues found on the surface of the cap

You Be the Microbiologist

DIRECTIONS: Scientists called **microbiologists** spend much of their time researching simple life forms. In this activity, you will learn about a type of organism that they might study. Decide which kind of simple life form you will research—bacteria, protist, or fungi. Then, choose a specific organism within that kingdom. Use the questions below to guide your research. Remember to use some of the simple-life-forms vocabulary words that you have learned. If you need additional space, continue your answers on a separate piece of paper.

1. Name of kingdom: _____

2. Name of organism: _____

3. Description of organism: _____

   _____

   _____

   _____

4. Where can this organism be found? _____

   _____

5. How is this organism different from plants and animals? What makes it unique?

   _____

   _____

   _____

6. How might this organism's environment be affected if the organism became extinct?

   _____

   _____

7. Additional facts: _____

   _____

   _____

8. Resources: _____

   _____

SIMPLE LIFE FORMS

Lichens, Mosses, and Algae

INQUIRY INVESTIGATION

A **lichen** is a special type of organism. It is a fungus, which is a heterotroph, that works with algae or autotrophic bacteria to survive. This type of relationship is called **mutualism**, when two organisms benefit by living together. The fungus receives its nutrients from the food that the algae or bacteria create. The algae or bacteria use the water and minerals that the fungus obtains from the ground.

Mosses can be found in many different places, such as in cracks in a sidewalk, near waterfalls, and on rocks in a forest. Moss is a type of **nonvascular plant**, which means that it does not have a system of tubes to transport water and nutrients. Therefore, these plants do not grow very tall.

Algae are plantlike protists. There are many types of algae. Some live in the ocean, while others can be found in the soil. The green algae on the surfaces of ponds and streams and in aquariums are important sources of food and oxygen for their environments.

DIRECTIONS: In this activity, you will compare lichens, moss, and algae.

MATERIALS

hand lens or microscope

microscope slides and cover slips

small, resealable plastic bags

craft stick

samples of lichens, mosses, and algae

PROCEDURE:

1. Collect a small sample of lichens and moss from the schoolyard. Place each sample in a resealable plastic bag. Record where you found each type of organism.

   Lichens _____

   Mosses _____

2. Collect a sample of algae from an aquarium by scraping the sides of the tank with a craft stick. Or, you might find algae at the edges of a local pond. Place the algae in a resealable plastic bag.

3. Examine each sample with a hand lens. Or, if it is available, prepare a slide to view the organism under a microscope.

4. Sketch a picture and write a short description of each organism in the charts on page 52.

LICHENS, MOSSES, AND ALGAE (CONTINUED)

Lichen Drawing	Moss Drawing	Algae Drawing

Description of Lichens	Description of Mosses	Description of Algae

1. Describe how the lichens, mosses, and algae are similar. How are they different?

_____

_____

_____

2. What evidence did you find that each organism is alive?

_____

_____

_____

Name: _____   Date: _____

Life as a One-Celled Organism

DIRECTIONS: Many organisms spend their lives as single cells. You may have observed a single-celled organism from pond water through a microscope, or you may have seen a picture of one in a science book. Imagine that you are a single-celled organism that lives in a pond. What kind of organism are you? What do you do during your days and nights in the pond? One day, you are collected in a jar by a scientist. Why did the scientist need water from the pond? Will you survive being taken from your environment? Will you make it back to the pond? Write a short story about these questions below.

_____

_____

_____

_____

_____

_____

_____

_____

_____

_____

_____

_____

_____

_____

_____

_____

_____

_____

Name: _____ Date: _____

SIMPLE LIFE FORMS

How Well Do Household Cleaners Work?

GRAPHING AND ANALYZING DATA

DIRECTIONS: Read the information and study the data chart below. Create a bar graph using the data in the chart. Then, use the data and graph to answer the questions below on a separate piece of paper.

Judy works in a hospital. Her job is to make sure that all of the areas are clean and disinfected. She is trying a new type of cleaner and wants to study how well it destroys bacteria colonies on different surfaces. First, she found the average number of bacteria in four areas of the hospital. Then, she cleaned each area and found out how many bacteria colonies were left in each location.

Number of Bacteria Colonies		
Surface	**Before**	**After**
Kitchen Counter	2,000	1,200
Kitchen Sink	3,500	3,000
Bathtub	10,000	8,000
Bathroom Counter	1,400	600

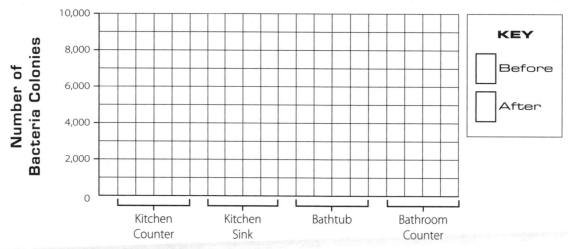

1. Does the cleaner show evidence of reducing the number of bacteria on all of the surfaces?

2. What percentage of bacteria was destroyed in the bathtub?

3. How many bacteria colonies were destroyed on the kitchen counter?

4. What is the total number of bacteria colonies that were destroyed?

5. Based on the data, where was the cleaner most effective in destroying bacteria? Use quantitative (numbers) data to support your answer.

Learning about the Plant Kingdom

DIRECTIONS: Context clues help us learn new words when we read. Use the words, phrases, and sentences around new words to determine their meanings. Look at the words in the chart and fill in the column "What I Think It Means." Read the passage and look for context clues to help determine the meanings of the words. Then, fill in the last column, "What It Means in Context." If your answer in the first column was completely correct, use the second column to add something to the word's meaning beyond your original ideas.

Word	What I Think It Means	What It Means in Context
vascular		
nonvascular		
conifers		
annual		
perennial		

Plants make up one of the major kingdoms of living things on Earth. They can be divided into two groups— **vascular** and **nonvascular**. A vascular plant has a system of tubes that carry water and nutrients from the roots to the leaves. Nonvascular plants are much smaller, without tubes to carry water. They absorb water and pass it from cell to cell.

Plants are further divided into more specific groups. For example, many plants are flowering plants, but those plants that produce cones instead of flowers are called **conifers**. These cones produce pollen and seeds, but unlike a flowering plant, a fruit does not protect a conifer's seeds.

Another way to divide types of plants is to use the lengths of their life spans. An **annual** is a plant that completes its life cycle within a growing season. It does not regrow each year, except through seeding new plants. A **perennial** is a plant that lives year after year, usually producing new growth and flowers during the spring. Perennials often have woody stems that help them survive harsh winter temperatures.

A Kingdom of Plants

DIRECTIONS: Find the plant vocabulary words in the word search below. Words can be found down, across, and diagonally. Then, on a separate piece of paper, write sentences for five of the words.

WORD BANK

annual	chlorophyll	cone-bearing plants	chloroplast
parachute	conifer	germination	pollination
phototropism	deciduous	perennial	spore
geotropism	flowering plants	photosynthesis	transpiration

```
B X C E N F P H O T O S Y N T H E S I S
S Z G O E V T R A N S P I R A T I O N Q
C C C Z N F Y I B V P E B G T O E K A I
P O H Z P I M M U W T A M J Q T E X C H
A N L Z M G F C C U S B M J F E F Z S Q
L E O G Q E D E H F R U I L Z P U M F J
A B R L K O S C R B N O U R Y K H L L D
H E O M X T A S I G E R M I N A T I O N
Y A P K E R W J C P D C Y M L C D D W P
G R L I A O D L S R M F V L H E P D E H
D I A P Q P O R X P P N Y C J P O E R O
E N S V L I X H F E O H W F D F L T I T
C G T U D S Y F M C P R I A K A L V N O
I P X G T M X H C O D S E Q B N I H G T
D L J B Z Z P E R E N N I A L N N K P R
U A K H H M U O C V L J T E A U A W L O
O N P A D C L I T D B H J R V A T E A P
U T Z E R H C G C L V L J T D L I A N I
S S H X C P I W G W U Q H I A N O D T S
J B F J K T V Q C E I G M E G S N O S M
```

A Kingdom of Plants

CROSSWORD PUZZLE

DIRECTIONS: Complete the crossword puzzle.

ACROSS

4. this type of woody plant sheds its leaves at the beginning of the cold season

6. green-colored substance that helps plants use sunlight for photosynthesis

8. the process by which a plant releases water from its leaves

9. the process that occurs when water enters a seed, it loses its seed coat, and releases a root and stem

DOWN

1. a response of a plant to light

2. the process in which birds and insects move pollen grains from one flower to another, enabling reproduction

3. attachment on a flying seed that allows it to be carried a far distance from the parent plant

5. seedlike object that falls from a fern and will grow into a new fern

6. type of plant that produces seeds and pollen on a cone

7. a response of a plant to gravity

Parts of Vascular Plants

DIRECTIONS: Use the words in the word bank to label the vascular plant diagram. Then, match each word to its description.

WORD BANK

roots	stem	leaves	seeds	flower

1. _____

2. _____

3. _____

4. _____

5. _____

6. _____ flat structures that contain cells that absorb the sunlight needed to perform photosynthesis

7. _____ produces seeds and attracts insects to help with pollination

8. _____ carries water and nutrients from the roots to the leaves and flowers

9. _____ found below the ground; take in water and often store nutrients

10. _____ created by the flower for reproduction

Comparing Plants

DIRECTIONS: Use the abbreviations for the types of plant listed in the word bank to fill in the blanks for the descriptions below. Some descriptions of plants will have more than one answer.

WORD BANK

ferns (F)	cone-bearing plants (CB)	flowering plants (FP)

1. _____ have vascular systems that transport water, minerals, and sugars throughout the plants

2. _____ seedless plants that include club mosses and horsetails

3. _____ have leaves that are called fronds, which are divided into many small parts that look like tiny leaves

4. _____ have seeds that are protected by fruits

5. _____ include maple, oak, and apple trees

6. _____ have reproductive cells, called spores, that are produced underneath the fronds

7. _____ create seeds for reproduction

8. _____ produce seeds on scaly structures called cones

9. _____ pollination is aided by the wind or insects

10. _____ include spruce, hemlock, and pine trees

11. _____ have seeds that are unprotected or "naked"

12. _____ have cells with cell walls and chloroplasts

13. _____ perform photosynthesis to produce food

14. _____ include tulips, daisies, and sunflowers

15. _____ are called evergreens; keep their needles all year round

THE PLANT KINGDOM

Getting the Seeds Out

FILL IN THE BLANKS

DIRECTIONS: Plants produce seeds as a method of reproduction. How does a plant use nature and other organisms to **disperse**, or spread, its seeds to new locations? Write the method of dispersion used by each type of plant from the word bank next to each type of seed below.

WORD BANK

wind	mammals	birds	water

1. coconut _____

2. cocklebur _____

3. holly _____

4. cherry _____

5. hickory nut _____

6. acorn _____

7. walnut _____

8. maple _____

9. pine _____

10. milkweed _____

11. How does a plant benefit from dispersing its seeds? What might happen if the seeds were not dispersed far from the plant?

_____

_____

Name: _____ Date: _____

What Is Inside a Seed?

If you opened a seed, what do you think you would see? Most seeds have three parts—a **seed coat**, an **embryo**, and a **cotyledon**.

DIRECTIONS: Use the words in the word bank to label the two seed diagrams. Then, match each word to its definition.

WORD BANK

seed coat	embryo	cotyledon

bean seed

pine seed

1. _____

2. _____

3. _____

4. _____

5. _____

6. _____

7. _____ a young plant

8. _____ a seed leaf that stores food for the embryo

9. _____ the hard, outer covering of the seed; protects the embryo and its food from drying out

Name: _____ Date: _____

When Seeds Fly

Plants cannot move around to spread their seeds, so they depend on animals, insects, water, and wind to **disperse** their seeds to fertile places where they can grow into new plants. In this activity, you will simulate how seeds are carried by wind to new locations.

WORD BANK

dandelions or milkweed	masking tape
dark construction paper	electric fan

PROCEDURE:

1. Designate one area of the classroom as the place where the original plant is "planted". Mark this area with masking tape. Place the fan on a desk behind this area. If an electric fan is not available, you can disperse the seeds with your breath by blowing on the plant's seed head.

2. Clear a path in the direction that the "wind" (fan or human breath) will blow.

3. Spread out 12 pieces of construction paper at different distances in front of the fan. Use tape to secure them to the floor. These represent "fertile" areas where seeds can survive and grow.

4. Make a prediction of how many seeds will land in a fertile area. Record this on the data chart on page 63.

5. Hold a dandelion or milkweed in front of the fan. Turn on the fan and let the seeds blow away. Turn off the fan when all of the seeds have blown off the seed head.

6. Carefully count the seeds that landed on the pieces of construction paper. Count the seeds that landed in other areas. Add these two numbers together to find the total number of seeds. Record this data on the data chart on page 63.

7. Clean up the seeds. Repeat steps 4 and 5 two additional times.

8. To calculate the percentage of seeds that landed on the paper in each trial, divide the number of seeds that landed on the paper by the total number of seeds and then multiply the quotient by 100. Record this on the data chart on page 63.

	Trial 1	Trial 2	Trial 3
Prediction: Number of Seeds That Will Land on Paper			
Number of Seeds That Landed on Paper			
Number of Seeds That Landed in Other Locations			
Total Number of Seeds			
Percentage of Seeds That Landed on Paper			

1. Why was the plant kept in one specific area?

_____

_____

2. Why were some areas "fertile" and others were not?

_____

_____

3. What percentage of your flying seeds had a chance to germinate? Explain.

_____

_____

4. Observe the same type of plant outdoors. How was the indoor experiment different? How was it similar?

_____

_____

5. What other methods of seed transport are used by plants?

_____

_____

6. Why do you think plants produce more seeds than will actually germinate?

_____

_____

Name: _____ Date: _____

Growing Up, Growing Down

What does the word phototropism mean? The prefix *photo* means *a response to light*, and the suffix *tropism* describes how something grows in a certain direction. **Phototropism** is how plants grow toward light.

DIRECTIONS: In the pictures below, draw how a plant might grow in response to each type of light source. Describe your drawing on the blank lines below each picture.

 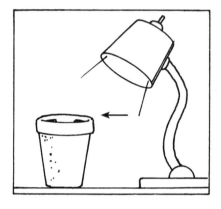 

_____   _____   _____

_____   _____   _____

_____   _____   _____

_____   _____   _____

Geotropism is similar to phototropism. But, instead of the shoot growing toward light, the roots of plants respond to the force of gravity. In which direction do you think that they grow?

DIRECTIONS: Complete the illustration of the germinating seed below. Draw the roots and shoot that would emerge from the seed and how they might grow in response to gravity. Describe your drawing below. On a separate piece of paper, write a procedure that you could follow to demonstrate geotropism.

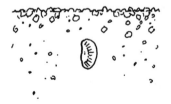

_____

_____

_____

_____

You Be the Botanist

DIRECTIONS: Scientists called **botanists** spend much of their time researching plants. In this activity, you can learn about some of the plants that botanists study. Choose one of the following six biomes: desert, tundra, deciduous forest, rain forest, freshwater pond, or ocean. Then, select a species of plant that is found there. Use the questions below to guide your research. Remember to use some of the plant-kingdom vocabulary words that you have learned. If you need additional space, continue your answers on a separate piece of paper.

1. Type of habitat: _____

2. Name of plant species: _____

3. Description of plant habitat: _____

   _____

   _____

4. Description of plant: _____

   _____

   _____

   _____

   _____

5. What adaptations and features make this plant unique? _____

   _____

   _____

   _____

6. How might the habitat be affected if this plant became extinct? _____

   _____

   _____

7. Resources: _____

   _____

   _____

Year After Year

DIRECTIONS: Fill in the blanks to complete the sentences below. Circle the designated letter or letters in each answer. Then, unscramble the circled letters to reveal the mystery word.

WORD BANK

producers	roots	nonvascular	niche
evergreen	annual	needles	seed

1. _____ Plants are _____ because they use sunlight to create their own food. (first and ninth letters)

2. _____ The needles of an _____ remain green even in the winter. (third letter)

3. _____ A plant's _____ absorb water and nutrients from the soil. (first letter)

4. _____ A plant that completes its entire life cycle in one year is called an _____. (third letter)

5. _____ A _____ is the first step in the life cycle of a plant. (second letter)

6. _____ _____ plants pass nutrients between their cells, instead of through a system of tubes. (first and fifth letters)

7. _____ A tree with _____ instead of leaves collects less ice and snow during a winter storm. (fifth letter)

8. _____ All plants have specific characteristics that help them fill a _____ in an ecosystem. (second letter)

MYSTERY WORD

Plants, such as trees and bulbs, that regrow new leaves and flowers each spring are called

__ __ __ __ __ __ __ __ __ .

Plant Reproduction

DIRECTIONS: Answer the following math problems. Use the space below each problem or a separate piece of paper to show your work.

1. Eric has 6 packages of seeds from last year. The directions say that only half of them will grow if they are not used the first year. There are 18 seeds in each package. If he wants to grow at least 25 sunflowers, how many packages of seeds should he use?

   Answer: _____

2. Ashley has several milkweed plants in her flower bed. Each plant has about 6 seedpods. Each pod contains about 48 seeds. If there are a total of 1,152 seeds, how many milkweed plants are there?

   Answer: _____

3. A fern reproduces by dispersing spores. About half of the spores will grow into new ferns. There are about 80 spores on the back of each stalk on the fern. If 120 new ferns have grown this year, how many stalks did the original plant have?

   Answer: _____

4. Trey's family planted 210 tulip bulbs last year. They did not dig them up, even though some will not survive from year to year. If $2/3$ of the bulbs regrow the second year, how many tulip plants will come up?

   Answer: _____

5. A dandelion produced 24 seeds. The seeds can fly up to $1/2$ mile (0.8 km) away from the original plant. What is the total distance that all of the seeds together could fly?

   Answer: _____

6. Vegetables in the school's garden will feed needy families. There are 12 families of 4 people. If each squash plant produces 24 squash, how many plants will produce enough for each person to have 4 squash?

   Answer: _____

Graphing Plant Growth

DIRECTIONS: After scientists record data from an experiment, they often create **graphs** to show pictures of their data. Create a graph using the data in the charts below. Decide whether the graph you create should be a line or bar graph. Remember to give the graph an appropriate title. Then, answer the questions about each set of data.

PART 1: Julie grew sunflowers in her garden. Before she cut the flowers to harvest the seeds, she measured the height of each plant.

Plant	Final Height of Sunflowers (cm)
A	58 cm
B	64 cm
C	89 cm
D	96 cm
E	65 cm

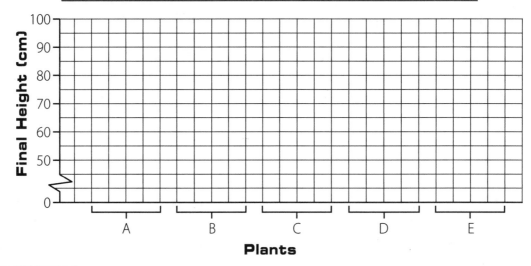

1. What is the average height of the sunflowers?

_____

2. What is the difference in height between the tallest and shortest sunflowers?

_____

3. What are some possible reasons that Plant D grew taller than Plant A?

_____

_____

PART 2: Daniel wanted to grow sunflowers in his garden. He planted the seeds in May. During the month of July, he measured the plants every five days. The data in the chart below shows the growth of one plant.

Date	Height of Sunflower (cm)
July 1	34 cm
July 6	36 cm
July 11	37 cm
July 16	39 cm
July 21	45 cm
July 26	48 cm
July 31	52 cm

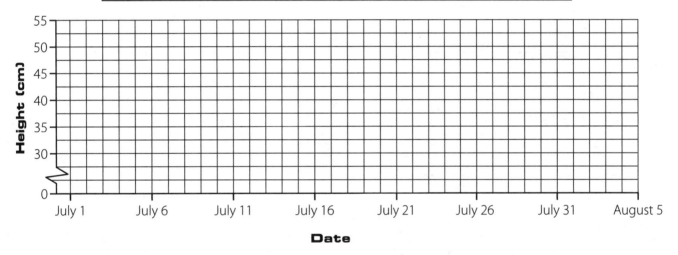

Date

4. How many centimeters did the sunflower grow throughout July?

   _____

5. About what height was the sunflower on July 13?

   _____

6. If Daniel continues to record the height of the sunflower in August, what height do you predict that the sunflower will be on August 5?

   _____

   _____

7. Graph your prediction of the height of the sunflower on August 5 using a dotted line.

Learning about the Animal Kingdom

CONTEXT CLUES

DIRECTIONS: Context clues help us learn new words when we read. Use the words, phrases, and sentences around new words to determine their meanings. Look at the words in the chart and fill in the column "What I Think It Means." Read the passage and look for context clues to help determine the meanings of the words. Then, fill in the last column, "What It Means in Context." If your answer in the first column was completely correct, use the second column to add something to the word's meaning beyond your original ideas.

Word	What I Think It Means	What It Means in Context
heterotrophs		
tissues		
invertebrates		
carnivores		
omnivores		

Are you interested in studying animals? If you are, there is a lot of work to do. There are more than one million different species of animals that scientists have discovered, and there could be millions more about which they do not know. All animals need three basic things to survive: food, water, and oxygen. Animals are **heterotrophs**, which means that they eat other organisms for food.

All animals are made up of many cells that work together so that animals can grow, reproduce, and survive. These cells are grouped together into different types of tissues. **Tissues** are groups of similar cells that work together to do certain jobs. Some animals are made up of only tissues, while other animals have tissues that combine into organs and organ systems.

Scientists can divide animals into two major groups. **Invertebrates**, the first group, do not have backbones. Some invertebrates, such as clams and insects, have hard shells or coverings that protect their organs. Other invertebrates, such as sea anemones, do not have hard coverings. Animals that have backbones, such as humans, dogs, and birds, are called vertebrates.

Animals move in many different ways. Some animals swim, while others fly. Some catch food with their claws, while others grab it with their mouths. Some animals, like fish and birds, move around; others, such as barnacles, swim around when they are young but then stay in one place for the rest of their lives. Animals get food in different ways, too. Some animals are **carnivores**, which means that they eat other animals. Others are herbivores and eat only plants. Animals called **omnivores** eat both plants and animals.

Name: _____ Date: _____

The Diversity of Animals

DIRECTIONS: Find the animal-kingdom vocabulary words in the word search below. Words can be found down, across, and diagonally. Then, on a separate piece of paper, write sentences for five of the words.

WORD BANK

reptiles	arthropods	zoology	carnivores	habitat	life cycle
amphibians	invertebrates	migration	crustaceans	hibernation	mollusks
instinct	arachnids	birds	mammals	insects	vertebrates

```
I  L  I  F  E  C  Y  C  L  E  Q  Y  K  T  Q  O  V  D  U  R
U  W  Q  A  B  M  O  I  D  U  Q  V  H  A  B  I  T  A  T  L
W  I  V  T  D  N  X  V  Y  I  T  N  M  J  S  L  P  E  W  G
K  J  L  V  E  R  T  E  B  R  A  T  E  S  Z  M  R  Q  N  S
K  Q  P  T  T  X  E  Z  U  G  G  A  I  D  H  B  I  R  D  S
I  N  S  E  C  T  S  K  R  D  J  O  S  O  R  T  X  O  E  F
H  G  G  Q  Y  L  A  D  R  Z  H  N  M  Q  F  A  D  T  J  K
I  F  H  T  X  H  W  M  H  N  A  N  X  S  Z  X  A  A  F  G
B  Y  V  B  K  Z  N  J  P  E  W  H  E  T  O  R  C  R  Q  B
E  M  A  M  M  A  L  S  C  H  Y  L  C  A  B  T  N  T  M  T
R  W  X  J  L  F  A  A  P  S  I  N  J  E  A  T  Z  H  A  A
N  X  Q  R  P  Q  T  U  D  T  I  B  T  J  H  V  O  R  D  R
A  G  G  G  T  S  Z  W  P  T  B  R  I  S  D  C  O  O  A  A
T  M  A  V  U  O  E  E  S  N  E  B  D  A  X  B  L  P  T  C
I  H  A  R  D  E  R  N  Z  V  M  V  N  O  N  W  O  O  H  H
O  U  C  F  M  Y  I  Z  N  K  M  H  K  N  J  S  G  D  I  N
N  X  J  M  A  C  Q  I  I  X  G  Z  X  D  O  J  Y  S  J  I
W  R  Y  I  Q  L  O  Y  K  E  M  O  L  L  U  S  K  S  P  D
Q  G  C  A  R  N  I  V  O  R  E  S  L  J  Q  L  M  W  Z  S
S  U  V  M  Y  Y  M  I  G  R  A  T  I  O  N  S  E  S  E  E
```

So Many Different Animals

DIRECTIONS: Match the words in the word bank to their definitions below.

WORD BANK

amphibians	arthropods	insects	mollusks
zoology	hibernation	birds	reptiles
mammals	arachnids	crustaceans	fish

1. _____ invertebrates with soft bodies; some have shells; include octopuses, snails, and clams

2. _____ spend part of life underwater, part of life on land; include frogs, toads, and salamanders

3. _____ invertebrates that have exoskeletons, two-part segmented bodies, and eight jointed legs each

4. _____ the largest animal phylum; make up three-fourths of all known living and fossil organisms; include insects, spiders, and crustaceans

5. _____ warm-blooded vertebrates that have wings, feathers, and beaks

6. _____ invertebrates that have exoskeletons, jointed legs, and two pairs of antennae each; most live in water, some live on land; include crabs, shrimp, and lobsters

7. _____ warm-blooded vertebrates that have hair or fur and give birth to live young; include dogs, horses, and humans

8. _____ cold-blooded vertebrates that live in water; breathe using gills; include bass, carp, and trout

9. _____ cold-blooded vertebrates that have scales, breathe air, and lay eggs; include snakes, lizards, and crocodiles

10. _____ the study of animals

11. _____ arthropods that have exoskeletons, three-part bodies, and three pairs of jointed legs each; some have wings; include ants, beetles, and grasshoppers

12. _____ when an animal goes into a deep sleep for the winter

Organization of Organisms

DIRECTIONS: Match each term with its definition. Then, for each picture below, write a sentence telling whether each organism has cells, tissues, and/or organs.

1. _____ cells

2. _____ tissues

3. _____ organs

4. _____ organ system

a. the basic units of structure in all living things

b. different types of tissues that work together to perform a job

c. organs that work together to help an organism function

d. groups of similar cells that work together to perform a job

5. An amoeba has _____

_____

_____

_____

6. A flower has _____

_____

_____

_____

7. A cat has _____

_____

_____

_____

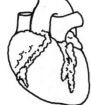

8. A human heart has _____

_____

_____

_____

THE ANIMAL KINGDOM

Observing Animal Objects

INQUIRY INVESTIGATION

When animals climb trees, fly through the air, or dig tunnels in the ground, they often leave pieces of evidence that show that they were there. Can you make inferences about why an animal would leave an object behind? An **inference** is an explanation based on facts that you already know.

MATERIALS

hand lens	scale (optional)	cicada skin
ruler	feathers	insect wing
colorful pencils	snakeskin	seashell

PROCEDURE:

1. Use the hand lens to closely observe an animal object from the materials list closely. Draw the object in the box below. Use colorful pencils to color the drawing.

2. Use a ruler to measure the length, width, and height of the object. Record the data below. If a scale is available, find the mass of the object and record it below. Write several other observations about the animal object in the space provided.

3. Make an inference about why the animal left the object behind.

4. Choose two other animal objects and record your observations in the charts on page 75.

Object: _____

Length: _____

Width: _____

Height: _____

Other observations: _____

_____

_____

Why do you think the animal left this object behind?

_____

_____

_____

_____

Object: _____

[ ]

Length: _____

Width: _____

Height: _____

Other observations: _____

_____

_____

Why do you think the animal left this object behind?

_____

_____

_____

_____

Object: _____

[ ]

Length: _____

Width: _____

Height: _____

Other observations: _____

_____

_____

Why do you think the animal left this object behind?

_____

_____

_____

_____

Life Cycle of a Frog

DIRECTIONS: Use the words in the word bank to label the frog life cycle below. Then, number the stages of the frog life cycle in the correct order, starting with an egg mass.

WORD BANK

frog	embryo	froglet
tadpole with hind legs	tadpole with hind and forelegs	spawn (egg mass)

1. _____

2. _____

3. _____

4. _____

5. _____

6. _____

_____ The tadpole becomes more frog-like. The tail becomes even smaller, and the legs continue to grow. The lungs can breathe air.

_____ The tadpole grows hind legs. It grows forelegs soon after. Its tail becomes smaller. Its lungs begin to develop to help it breathe air on land.

_____ An embryo forms in the egg mass. Organs and gills begin to form.

_____ The frog has lungs that are fully developed and lives on land most of the time. It eats insects and worms. It will find a mate and reproduce.

_____ After 21 days, the embryo leaves the egg mass and develops into a tadpole. The tadpole has a long tail. The tadpole will eat small plants. It also uses plants as camouflage from predators.

_____ A female frog lays a large clump of eggs, called spawn, in the water. The egg mass is too large and slippery to be eaten by other animals.

Life Cycle of a Butterfly

LABELING AND SEQUENCING

DIRECTIONS: Use the words in the word bank to label the butterfly life cycle below. Then, number the stages of the butterfly life cycle in the correct order, starting with an egg.

WORD BANK

| caterpillar | chrysalis | egg | butterfly |

1. _____

2. _____

3. _____

4. _____

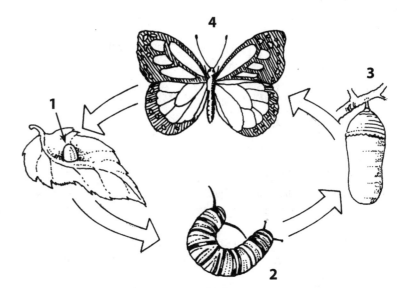

_____ In about 10–12 days, a butterfly emerges from the chrysalis.

_____ A larva (caterpillar) hatches from the egg in 3–5 days. The larva will eat the egg case and the milkweed leaves.

_____ A single egg is laid by an adult monarch butterfly and is attached to a milkweed leaf.

_____ The larva **molts**, or sheds its outer skin as it grows. Soon, it will stop eating and find a safe place to pupate. The larva molts for the last time. Its new skin dries and hardens into a jade green chrysalis.

Name: _____ Date: _____

DIRECTIONS: All vertebrates are placed in the phylum **Chordata** because they have backbones. Match each animal to its description below.

WORD BANK

hummingbird	moray eel	bullfrog
chameleon	rattlesnake	tiger salamander

1. I am cold-blooded and breathe oxygen through a pair of gills.

My fins help me swim quickly through water. My body is covered with scales.

I usually catch prey while I am hiding between rocks and in coral reefs.

Who am I? _____

2. I am cold-blooded. I spent my early life in water, where I breathed through gills.

When I became an adult, I developed a pair of lungs and moved onto land. Females of my species return to the water to lay their eggs.

I have powerful hind-leg muscles for jumping long distances.

Who am I? _____

3. I am a cold-blooded amphibian. I keep my tail when I become an adult.

Females of my species lay their eggs in water.

Some members of my species spend their entire lives in water; others live on land.

Who am I? _____

4. I am cold-blooded and have lungs for breathing and thick, scaly skin that helps me prevent losing water.

I can change the color of my skin to blend in with my environment.

I have a sticky tongue for grabbing insects.

Who am I? _____

5. I am cold-blooded and have a long, thin body that can bend and curve.

I move by contracting muscles that are attached to my ribs and backbones.

I am a carnivore; I eat mice and other rodents. My hollow teeth inject venom into my prey.

Who am I? _____

6. I am warm-blooded, and my body is covered in feathers.

Female members of my species lay eggs instead of giving live birth.

I can beat my wings 10–15 times per second.

Who am I? _____

Name: _____ Date: _____

Invertebrate Animals

DIRECTIONS: Invertebrates are animals that do not have backbones. They are covered by hard exoskeletons, have shells, or have no covering at all. Match each animal to its description below.

WORD BANK

| clam | coral | sponge | roundworm | snail | jellyfish |

1. I am classified into the phylum Porifera, which means "having pores."

Members of my species have irregular shapes and lack the tissues and organs that most other animals have.

We have been on Earth for 540 million years. You might use a real one of us in the shower or a fake one to wash your dishes.

Who am I? _____

2. I am classified into the phylum Cnidaria, which means "stinging cells."

Members of my species use stinging cells both to capture prey and for defense.

Some members of my species look like transparent bubbles.

Who am I? _____

3. I am classified into the phylum Cnidaria and have a vaselike shape.

As a young larva, I attached to a solid surface, such as a broken shell or sunken ship.

I do not move around. I combine with other members of my species to build huge reefs in the ocean.

Who am I? _____

4. I am classified into the phylum Mollusca and have a soft body that is protected by a hard outer shell.

I have gills that enable me to breathe by removing oxygen from the water.

I can hide in my shell when I am threatened by predators. I am a scavenger who feeds on decaying material.

Who am I? _____

5. I am classified into the phylum Mollusca.

I have two shells that are held together by a hinge and strong muscles.

I use a thin foot muscle to burrow into the sand and mud. Members of my species are eaten as seafood by humans.

Who am I? _____

6. I am classified into the phylum Nematoda. All members of my species have long, cylinder-like, smooth bodies.

I can regenerate, or regrow, body parts.

I have a brain and sense organs that detect food, light, and predators. I spend my life burrowing in the soil.

Who am I? _____

INVERTEBRATE ANIMALS (CONTINUED)

WORD BANK

sea urchin   crawfish   octopus   spider   butterfly   starfish

7. I am classified into the phylum Mollusca.

I have eight tentacles with suckers that help me sense my environment. My tentacles also help me capture prey.

Although I am a mollusk, I do not have an external shell.

I have a large brain and am highly intelligent.

Who am I? _____

8. I am classified into the phylum Arthropoda. All members of my phylum have exoskeletons, which are hard, waterproof skeletons on the outside of our bodies.

As I grow, I will molt, or shed my exoskeleton.

My antennae contain my sense organs. My first pair of legs has claws for capturing prey and for defense.

Who am I? _____

9. I am classified into the phylum Arthropoda. I have two body sections—my head/chest and my abdomen.

I have eight legs. My hollow fangs inject venom into prey.

Some members of my species spin sticky webs to capture prey, while others chase their prey.

Who am I? _____

10. I am classified into the phylum Arthropoda.

I have three body sections and six legs. My wings and legs are attached to my thorax, or middle section.

I have a pair of compound eyes, which helps me watch for predators.

Once in my life, I go through a metamorphosis, which is a change in my body structure.

Who am I? _____

11. I am classified into the phylum Echinodermata, which means "spiny skin."

I have tube feet beneath each of my five arms, which help me move on the ocean floor and capture food.

I can regenerate, or regrow, parts of my body that I have lost.

I eat mollusks, crabs, and other echinoderms.

Who am I? _____

12. I am classified into the phylum Echinodermata. I have movable spines that cover and protect my body.

I use my spines to dig into cracks between rocks to hide from predators. You might think that I look like a pincushion.

To eat, I scrape algae, chew seaweed, and crush pieces of coral with five strong teeth.

Who am I? _____

Name: _____   Date: _____

What Animals Need to Survive

DIRECTIONS: All animals need food, water, and shelter. Think of some animals that you have seen. How do their environments provide these necessities for them? Fill in the chart below with your observations.

Animal	Type of Food	Source of Water	Shelter
1. box turtle			
2. cardinal			
3. bullfrog			
4. goose			
5. squirrel			

Now, imagine what might happen to these animals if humans destroyed their habitats. Fill in the chart below with ways that humans can provide resources for these animals that are taken away from them by new construction and development.

Animal	Type of Food	Source of Water	Shelter
6. box turtle			
7. cardinal			
8. bullfrog			
9. goose			
10. squirrel			

THE ANIMAL KINGDOM

You Be the Zoologist

INDEPENDENT RESEARCH

DIRECTIONS: Scientists called **zoologists** spend much of their time researching animals. In this activity, you can learn about some of the animals that zoologists study. Choose one group of vertebrate animals below. Then, select a specific animal that is found in that group of vertebrates. Use the following questions to guide your research. Remember to use some of the animal-kingdom vocabulary words that you have learned. If you need additional space, continue your answers on a separate piece of paper.

VERTEBRATES				
mammals	reptiles	amphibians	fish	birds

1. Group of vertebrates: _____

2. Name of vertebrate animal: _____

3. Description of animal: _____

   _____

   _____

   _____

4. What adaptations and features make this animal unique?_____

   _____

   _____

   _____

5. How would the animal's habitat be affected if this animal became extinct?

   _____

   _____

   _____

6. Resources: _____

   _____

Name: _____   Date: _____

Amazing Animal Facts

DIRECTIONS: Answer the following math problems. Use the space below each problem or a separate piece of paper to show your work.

1. There are 36 adult Canada geese living near a lake. If each pair of geese produces 12 eggs, what is the total number of eggs that the geese produce?

Answer: _____

2. The survival rate of sea turtles reaching maturity is only 1%. If 6 turtles each lay 200 eggs on the beach, how many of the eggs will hatch and grow into mature sea turtles?

Answer: _____

3. Monarch butterflies lay an average of 200 eggs at a time. If 32 monarchs laid their eggs in a backyard, how many monarch eggs would there be?

Answer: _____

4. Gray whales nurse from their mothers for up to 8 months. They drink about 50 gallons of milk per day. If there are 3 baby whales in the bay this year, what is the total amount of milk that they will drink before they stop nursing? Assume that each month has 30 days.

Answer: _____

5. A bat can eat at least 600 mosquitoes per night. If there are 12 bats living in the bat box, how many mosquitoes could they eat in one week?

Answer: _____

6. When a frog lays an egg, the single egg splits into two cells after about an hour. How many cells will there be after it splits 3 more times?

Answer: _____

7. Some species of snakes shed their skin about every 20 days. About how many times do they shed per year?

Answer: _____

8. Before they hibernate each winter, bears must eat extra food to gain weight. A bear might weigh 1,400 pounds before its hibernation begins. How much will it weigh after hibernation if it loses 20% of its total weight during its hibernation?

Answer: _____

Snakes in the Desert

DIRECTIONS: Use the data below to create a line graph of the snakes' body temperatures in the desert during a hot July day. Use a different color of pencil to graph each snake's body temperature. Then, answer the questions below.

Body Temperature		
Time	**Snake 1**	**Snake 2**
12 AM	12°C	12°C
2 AM	8°C	12°C
4 AM	8°C	14°C
6 AM	10°C	18°C
8 AM	18°C	20°C
10 AM	30°C	24°C
12 PM	35°C	24°C
2 PM	40°C	22°C
4 PM	30°C	20°C
6 PM	20°C	15°C
8 PM	12°C	12°C
10 PM	9°C	10°C
12 AM	9°C	8°C

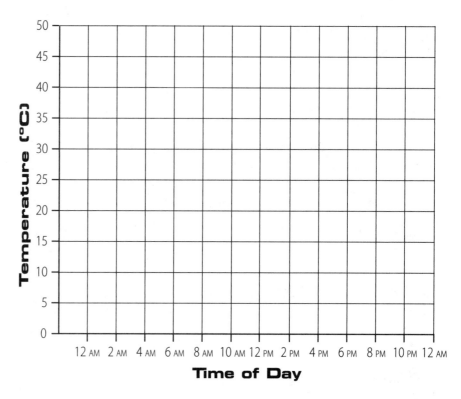

1. Why do you think the snakes' body temperatures changed during the day?

_____

_____

2. On this day, the weather was hot and sunny with a few clouds in the sky. Based on your graph of the two snakes' body temperatures, infer the location of each snake throughout the day.

_____

_____

_____

_____

Learning about the Human Body

DIRECTIONS: Context clues help us learn new words when we read. Use the words, phrases, and sentences around new words to determine their meanings. Look at the words in the chart and fill in the column "What I Think It Means." Read the passage and look for context clues to help determine the meanings of the words. Then, fill in the last column, "What It Means in Context." If your answer in the first column was completely correct, use the second column to add something to the word's meaning beyond your original ideas.

Word	What I Think It Means	What It Means in Context
organs		
circulatory		
respiratory		
digestive		
esophagus		
muscles		

Have you ever wondered what the inside of your body looks like? Underneath your skin, there are many different systems that work together to keep you alive. Each of these systems is made up of different **organs**, structures that do a specific job for the system. For example, your heart, an organ in the **circulatory** system, pumps blood to all of the different parts of your body. Imagine what might happen to your body if blood could not get to your feet, hands, or brain.

There are many other systems in your body. Each one is very important. The **respiratory** system brings oxygen into the lungs and gets rid of carbon dioxide. The lungs, trachea, and nose are organs in this system. The **digestive** system breaks down the food that you eat. After you chew and swallow food, it is pushed down the **esophagus** into the stomach, where powerful **muscles** crush the food into tiny pieces.

Your body is also very fragile. You should always wear protective gear when you ride your bike or skateboard. If you fall, you might break a bone. It is important to take care of your bones because some of them, such as your ribs and skull, protect important organs. Do you know which organs they protect?

Human Body Organs and Systems

W O R D   S E A R C H

DIRECTIONS: Find the human body organs and systems vocabulary words in the word search below. Words can be found down, across, and diagonally. Then, on a separate piece of paper, write sentences for five of the words.

WORD BANK

cell	digestive	circulatory	brain	small intestine
tissue	muscular	excretory	spinal cord	liver
organ	nervous	heart	blood	kidneys
organ system	immune	lungs	stomach	veins
skeletal	respiratory	skin	large intestine	arteries

```
Y F P I Q X K W K N N E X C R E T O R Y
C Y L U P Q P K A I C Z H S S D K S Z D
V G C C A Q Y G Y M G E S E S F Y J O L
S F A U Y G R M P X U E L G A N H O J A
J K F S I O C B N E I S N L E R L S S R
O T I S T R C S P R S U C E E B T I M G
F U L N C O K B E L L V J U L Z M T A E
S H R I V H M T T D X E X Y L E W I L I
I J A C D O R A R I Y I U R T A P S L N
E G R L I A M O C R A N T S N D R S I T
S W I W U R C U O H B S Y E I M M U N E
E C E V H L C T P K R S K J P D H E T S
J I S K A U A U B S N W B X K I L S E T
C W B N I R N V L A T N K I Z G D K S I
F C I C I D U E G A I R G T E E F E T N
I P X P P U N R R A T T A E D S J L I E
S M S Q P Y O E R V G O W L M T E E N E
G E T C V V X B Y N O H R T W I L T E I
R T Z L I V E R M S K U I Y E V Q A V F
M O N R C S C V V U U J S I D E K L A X
```

Organ Systems of the Human Body

M A T C H I N G / M A G I C   N U M B E R

DIRECTIONS: Match each definition with the correct human body system. Then, copy the number from each answer into the box below with the matching letter. When you add three numbers down, across, or diagonally, the sums should all be the same.

1. _____ made up of several types of organs that help the body perform different jobs

2. _____ allows the body to move

3. _____ breaks down food and absorbs nutrients

4. _____ helps protect the body from disease and infection

5. _____ controls the body's functions and senses the environment outside the body

6. _____ takes oxygen into the body and releases carbon dioxide

7. _____ supports the body and protects its internal organs

8. _____ uses blood to bring nutrients and oxygen to cells of the body

9. _____ removes wastes

a. muscular

b. excretory

c. immune

d. skeletal

e. nervous

f. digestive

g. respiratory

h. organ system

i. circulatory

a.	b.	c.
d.	e.	f.
g.	h.	i.

MAGIC NUMBER = _____

Name That Body System

DIRECTIONS: Each system of the body has a specific job. It works together with other body systems to keep the body healthy. Match each body system to its description below.

WORD BANK

| muscular | circulatory | digestive | skeletal | nervous | respiratory |

1. I bring supplies, such as food and oxygen, to cells. I also pick up wastes, such as carbon dioxide, from these cells and deliver them to the lungs.

I help fight diseases with special blood cells.

Some of my organs are the heart, arteries, and veins.

Who am I? _____

2. I take food into the body and break it down into smaller pieces. I also get rid of unused food materials.

I place nutrients in the blood stream, which carries them to all of the body's cells.

Some of my organs are the stomach, esophagus, large intestine, and small intestine.

Who am I? _____

3. One of my jobs is to protect the body's internal organs. I also produce red and white blood cells.

I give the body shape and work with muscles to help the body move, jump, and stand.

Some of my organs are the skull, femur, vertebrae, and rib cage.

Who am I? _____

4. One of my main jobs is to help the body move, walk, run, and stretch.

I also help blood move through the body, push food down the esophagus, and help the stomach crush food into smaller pieces.

Some of my organs are the stomach, heart, biceps, and triceps.

Who am I? _____

5. I take oxygen into the lungs. I place this oxygen in the blood stream.

I also remove carbon dioxide from the body.

Some of my organs are the lungs, trachea, nose, and mouth.

Who am I? _____

6. My main job is to help the body sense its environment. I also control all of the other systems of the body.

When the body comes into contact with hot objects, I use reflexes to prevent bodily injury.

Some of my organs include the brain, spinal cord, and nerves.

Who am I? _____

Name: _____   Date: _____

Human Organs and Organ Systems

CATEGORIZING

DIRECTIONS: Place a check mark in the box to show which body system each organ is a part of. Remember, an organ can work with several body systems.

Organ	Skeletal	Digestive	Muscular	Nervous	Immune	Respiratory	Circulatory	Excretory
skull								
femur								
vertebrae								
stomach								
intestines								
mouth								
esophagus								
kidneys								
eyes								
brain								
spinal cord								
nose								
skin								
lungs								
trachea								
epiglottis								
heart								
arteries								
capillaries								
veins								

Name: _____ Date: _____

HUMAN BODY SYSTEMS

How Does Exercise Affect Your Heart Rate?

INQUIRY INVESTIGATION

What causes your **pulse**? Each time the ventricles of the heart contract, or get smaller, blood is forced into the arteries. Each beat of the heart makes the arteries stretch, which causes the pulsing sensation that you feel. As blood is being pushed out of the heart with great force, it moves very quickly so that it can reach parts of the body that are far from the heart.

In this activity, you will find your pulse rate and calculate the number of times that your heart beats per minute. Then, you will look at the class data to see if boys and girls have different pulse rates.

PROCEDURE:

1. Sit in a chair and relax for 1 minute. Use your index and middle fingers to locate your pulse on your wrist or neck.

2. Count the number of times that you feel your pulse for 15 seconds. Multiply this number by 4. This will be your resting pulse rate for 1 minute. Record this number on the chart below.

3. Jog in place for 1 minute. After 1 minute, stop jogging and use your index and middle fingers to locate your pulse on your wrist or neck. Calculate your pulse rate as you did in step 2. Record this number in the Active Pulse Rate column.

4. Repeat steps 1–3 two additional times. Then, calculate your average heart rate by adding the three trials and dividing by 3.

Trial	Resting Pulse Rate	Active Pulse Rate
1		
2		
3		
Average		

5. Your teacher will create two columns on the board, one for boys and one for girls. Write your average resting and active pulse rates in the correct columns. Then, calculate the average pulse rate for boys and girls in your class. Do boys and girls have different pulse rates? How can you explain this?

_____

_____

_____

Name: _____ Date: _____

Amazing Human Body Math Facts

MATH SKILLS

DIRECTIONS: Answer the following math problems. Use the space below each problem or a separate piece of paper to show your work.

1. When the human brain is developing, it creates 250,000 neurons (brain cells) a minute. How many brain cells does it create in one day?

Answer: _____

2. The average human head weighs about 8 pounds. If an average man weighs 160 pounds, what percentage of his weight does his head make up?

Answer: _____

3. Average humans blink their eyes 6,205,000 times each year. If a person is awake for 16 hours a day, how many times will she blink a day? An hour? A minute?

Answers: _____

_____

_____

4. 15,000,000 blood cells are destroyed every second to make room for new blood cells. How many blood cells are destroyed every hour?

Answer: _____

5. An average human body is 80% water. How many pounds of water are found in a 150-pound human?

Answer: _____

6. During a 24-hour period, average humans will breathe 23,000 times. How many times will they breathe in one year? 20 years? 50 years?

Answers: _____

_____

_____

Digestion Math

DIRECTIONS: Food travels a long distance through the digestive system. Use the following information to create a bar graph. Then, answer the questions below.

Organ	Length (cm)
Mouth	7.5 cm
Esophagus	25 cm
Stomach	25 cm
Small intestine	600 cm
Large intestine	150 cm

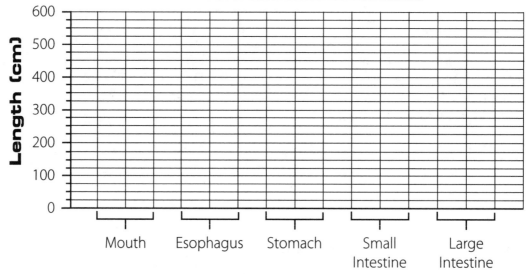

Organs

1. What is the total distance that food will travel through the digestive system?

   Answer: _____

2. What percentage of the distance in the digestive system does the small intestine make up?

   Answer: _____

3. What percentage of the distance in the digestive system does the large intestine make up?

   Answer: _____

4. How many times longer than the large intestine is the small intestine?

   Answer: _____

A Day in the Life of a Cell

CREATIVE WRITING

DIRECTIONS: Imagine that you are a single cell that is located somewhere in the human body. You might be a blood cell that moves throughout the blood vessels, a cell in the stomach that helps digest food, or a muscle cell in the leg of an athlete. Use science books, encyclopedias, or the Internet to help you write a first-person short story that describes what it would be like to live as one of these cells for a day. Remember to describe what you might see, hear, feel, and smell during your experience as a human body cell.

_____

_____

_____

_____

_____

_____

_____

_____

_____

_____

_____

_____

_____

_____

_____

_____

_____

_____

_____

_____

_____

_____

ADAPTATIONS

Learning about Adaptations

CONTEXT CLUES

DIRECTIONS: Context clues help us learn new words when we read. Use the words, phrases, and sentences around new words to determine their meanings. Look at the words in the chart and fill in the column "What I Think It Means." Read the passage and look for context clues to help determine the meanings of the words. Then, fill in the last column, "What It Means in Context." If your answer in the first column was completely correct, use the second column to add something to the word's meaning beyond your original ideas.

Word	What I Think It Means	What It Means in Context
diversity		
adaptations		
marine		
finches		
theory		

In December 1831, an English naturalist named Charles Darwin set sail on a British naval ship, the *HMS Beagle*. Over the next five years, Darwin traveled around the world, taking careful notes about everything that he saw. He noticed many types of plants and animals that were not found in England. He was amazed by the great **diversity**, or variety of plants and animals, that he saw.

After a few years on the boat, he arrived at the Galapagos Islands, a group of small islands off the west coast of South America. Darwin observed that many of the animals on the islands had special **adaptations** that helped them defend themselves and collect food. For example, he knew that most iguanas lived on land and had small claws to help them climb trees to eat leaves. On the Galapagos Islands, he found a species of iguana that lived in the ocean. The shape of this **marine** iguana's body and tail helped it swim underwater. It had special claws that were adapted to help it grab onto slippery rocks. Its rounded head helped it eat algae that grew close to the ocean floor.

Darwin also noticed differences in other types of animals. He saw that tortoises on each island had differently shaped shells. **Finches**, a type of bird, had differently shaped beaks. After observing the finches, he found that each bird's beak was adapted to eat certain types of food. When Darwin returned from his trip, his observations helped him develop an important scientific concept called the **theory** of evolution by natural selection.

Name: _____   Date: _____

Changes Over Time

DIRECTIONS: Find the adaptations vocabulary words in the word search below. Words can be found down, across, and diagonally. Then, on a separate piece of paper, write sentences for five of the words.

WORD BANK

adaptation	Charles Darwin	camouflage	evolution	species
variations	finches	extinct	natural selection	characteristics
structure	tortoises	endangered	theory	*HMS Beagle*

```
F  X  W  F  I  N  C  H  E  S  S  Y  A  S  J  O  X  M  R  I
N  J  K  M  H  C  Q  Q  W  Q  I  N  Z  X  Z  S  H  V  N  J
A  C  G  C  L  F  A  U  C  N  O  S  T  D  B  P  N  S  G  A
T  C  R  M  U  Q  V  M  R  E  N  D  A  N  G  E  R  E  D  G
U  H  K  W  O  X  U  A  O  O  Z  R  M  Y  U  C  X  D  Y  M
R  A  J  S  F  A  Q  X  I  U  W  Q  N  G  Q  I  A  K  Z  T
A  R  V  V  C  T  X  T  O  S  F  E  J  Q  O  E  C  H  V  S
L  A  H  X  O  Y  A  Y  E  V  S  L  X  F  H  S  I  X  H  C
S  C  J  W  K  I  V  S  N  W  V  T  A  T  D  L  Q  F  M  H
E  T  K  C  R  L  I  X  O  P  U  V  R  G  I  J  J  N  S  A
L  E  Z  A  N  O  A  C  D  P  W  K  I  U  E  N  Y  N  B  R
E  R  V  W  T  E  C  D  P  Z  W  J  B  Y  C  Q  C  I  E  L
C  I  P  R  E  V  M  E  A  U  Y  A  R  W  I  T  B  T  A  E
T  S  O  U  S  O  D  X  K  P  G  Z  S  F  Q  Q  U  K  G  S
I  T  W  S  E  L  N  J  I  Y  T  H  E  O  R  Y  H  R  L  D
O  I  V  X  P  U  A  J  U  R  D  A  B  J  Y  B  I  T  E  A
N  C  Z  X  I  T  Z  V  Z  S  J  W  T  H  N  X  D  J  C  R
C  S  Q  Z  N  I  K  G  I  I  W  K  L  I  U  Q  J  F  U  W
W  E  Z  J  A  O  U  T  N  Z  D  M  B  Q  O  W  K  Z  S  I
C  G  L  V  H  N  B  S  P  V  E  X  P  W  Q  N  A  A  F  N
```

Changes Over Time

Name: _____   Date: _____

DIRECTIONS: Complete the crossword puzzle.

ACROSS

1. the idea that organisms that are better adapted to their environments will survive and create new organisms of their species

4. differences between organisms

6. the ability of an organism to blend in with its surroundings

8. Darwin noticed that these organisms had differently shaped shells, based on the islands where they were found

10. a part of an organism that can be used for identification

11. Darwin noticed that these birds had differently shaped beaks that helped them eat certain types of food

DOWN

2. trait that helps an organism survive and reproduce

3. a group of similar organisms that can produce offspring (children)

5. gradual change of organisms over time

7. an idea that is based on many detailed observations

9. English naturalist; developed the theory of evolution by natural selection

Name: _____ Date: _____

Name the Animal Adaptation

MYSTERY WORDS

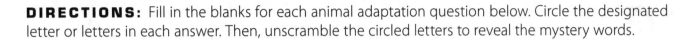

DIRECTIONS: Fill in the blanks for each animal adaptation question below. Circle the designated letter or letters in each answer. Then, unscramble the circled letters to reveal the mystery words.

WORD BANK

wallaroo	sea otter	koala	squirrel monkey
camel	bullfrog	hedgehog	red panda
giraffe	python	beaver	

1. _____ has spiny armor that protects it from predators and cushions its falls from trees (first letter)

2. _____ has long eyelashes and hair-lined ears that block blowing sand; can close its nostrils to keep sand out (second letter)

3. _____ uses specially designed hands and feet and a thick, padded tail to hold on to tree branches for long periods of time (second and third letters)

4. _____ does not have a blubber layer; air trapped in its fur keeps it warm and helps it float (first and fifth letters)

5. _____ has heat sensors on its upper lip to help it find prey (sixth letter)

6. _____ inflates its body with air when it's threatened (sixth and seventh letters)

7. _____ has valves that close its nose and ears when underwater; uses its large front teeth to cut and chew wood (fourth letter)

8. _____ has furry pads on its feet that help with rock climbing (second letter)

9. _____ can live many weeks without water; neck is adapted so that it can feed on high treetops (second letter)

10. _____ can leap through trees with great force due to the special design of its legs (ninth and eleventh letters)

11. _____ has wide teeth and powerful jaws for chewing tough bamboo leaves (sixth letter)

MYSTERY WORDS: This animal swallows its prey whole by opening its mouth extremely wide.

White-Throated __ __ __ __ __ __ __ __   __ __ __ __ __ __ __

ADAPTATIONS

More Than One Way to Hide

FILL IN THE BLANKS

DIRECTIONS: Animals use **camouflage** to protect themselves from predators or to hide when they hunt for prey. Use the chart below to fill in the blank with the type of camouflage each animal uses. You will use each type of camouflage more than once.

Type of Camouflage	How It Is Used
blending	the colors on an animal's body match its surroundings
patterns	the animal's markings make the outline of the animal's body hard to see
disguise	the animal hides in plain sight by looking like an object in its surroundings
mimicry	the animal imitates a harmful animal, making its enemies shy away
counter shading	the animal's body blends with the ground or the sky

1. _____ a walking stick holding on to a tree branch

2. _____ a group of zebras running through tall grass

3. _____ a longhorn beetle that looks like a wasp

4. _____ a chameleon sitting in a pile of leaves

5. _____ a giraffe running through a patch of trees

6. _____ a praying mantis sitting on a branch

7. _____ a moth with large round rings on its wings that look like eyes

8. _____ a hawk moth caterpillar's back that looks like a snake's head

9. _____ a spider hiding inside a flower

10. _____ a leopard frog sitting in shallow water

11. _____ a viceroy butterfly that looks like a bad-tasting monarch butterfly

12. _____ a polar bear sitting on ice

13. _____ a king snake that looks like a poisonous coral snake

14. _____ a lion hiding in the grass

15. _____ a penguin that will not be seen by a shark swimming under it because of the penguin's light underbelly

Name: _____   Date: _____

Plant Adaptations

DIRECTIONS: When most people think about adaptations, they think about animals. Have you ever thought about how plants **adapt**, or change to fit their environments? Match the method of adaptation with the name of the plant below.

1. _____ It produces many acorns, which are buried in the ground by squirrels. Acorns that are still in the ground in the spring sprout into new trees.

2. _____ Its roots can absorb oxygen from water.

3. _____ Its slimy, juicy tissue stores water in the dry season.

4. _____ Its stem has thorns that keep predators from eating its flowers.

5. _____ It produces many spores, which are dispersed by wind or water.

6. _____ It produces a poison that will harm animals that try to eat it.

7. _____ Its dark, fuzzy leaves absorb and store heat from the sun.

8. _____ Its slim needles allow heavy snow to fall through them.

9. _____ Its tiny leaves reduce the amount of water lost through transpiration.

10. _____ Its broad leaves repel water.

a. desert cactus

b. oak tree

c. rosebush in a garden

d. reed at the edge of a pond

e. milkweed

f. alpine on a cold mountain

g. fern

h. desert creosote shrub

i. pine tree on a tall mountain

j. mangrove tree

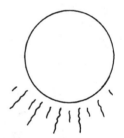

ADAPTATIONS

Bird Adaptations

INQUIRY INVESTIGATION

How are birds **physically adapted** to their environments? They have different structures that help them survive. Some birds have differently shaped beaks to eat specific of foods, while others have longer legs to stand in deep water while feeding. There are many different types of adaptations, like size, wing span, foot type, and feather shape. In this activity, you will create a model of a bird that is physically adapted to live in a specific habitat.

MATERIALS

different colors of clay	feathers	construction paper	cotton swabs
drinking straws	chenille craft sticks	buttons	any additional teacher-approved materials
twigs	small pebbles	scissors	

PROCEDURE:

1. Choose one of the habitats below.

    a. dry, sandy desert; very little water or plant life

    b. cold, mountainous area; very high elevation

    c. Antarctic region; snow and ice cover the ground all year

    d. tropical rain forest; full of colorful plant life

2. Use the provided materials to create a model of a bird that is physically adapted to survive in your chosen habitat.

3. Describe the bird's physical adaptations.

    _____

    _____

    _____

    _____

4. How might this bird species adapt if its habitat were changed by humans or nature?

    _____

    _____

    _____

    _____

Name: _____ Date: _____

Creating New Adaptations

CREATIVE WRITING

Over millions of years, many different species of plants and animals have adapted to their environments by developing characteristics that help them survive. For instance, mammals that live in cold, polar regions have developed thicker fur coats than animals that live in hot, tropical areas.

DIRECTIONS: Think of a plant or animal that is **native** to, or naturally found in, your area. Describe three adaptations that this plant or animal would need if it were to migrate to a different location with a different climate, vegetation, and food web. Then, draw before and after pictures of the plant or animal in the boxes below.

_____

_____

_____

_____

_____

_____

Before	**After**

Organisms in Danger

W O R D   S E A R C H

DIRECTIONS: Find the endangered and extinct organisms vocabulary words in the word search below. Words can be found down, across, and diagonally. Then, on a separate piece of paper, write sentences for five of the words.

WORD BANK

extinct	biodiversity	keystone	habitat destruction	grizzly bear
endangered	poaching	preservation	Atlantic salmon	species
threatened	captive breeding	fragmentation	bald eagle	native

```
D  N  B  I  O  D  I  V  E  R  S  I  T  Y  P  Q  T  W  O  U
A  V  U  I  E  N  D  A  N  G  E  R  E  D  W  I  T  J  V  O
M  H  R  B  A  L  D  E  A  G  L  E  A  V  B  D  N  K  Q  P
S  A  R  I  F  U  F  B  V  U  F  H  S  B  F  O  H  N  G  W
C  B  U  S  L  C  T  R  F  O  G  Q  X  P  M  I  O  R  K  U
A  I  T  F  H  N  O  J  A  Q  K  D  R  L  N  I  H  W  I  K
P  T  L  T  G  C  F  D  H  G  V  K  A  V  T  Y  S  U  J  W
T  A  L  Q  F  K  Y  B  W  V  M  S  M  A  D  G  D  X  Z  K
I  T  K  E  Y  S  T  O  N  E  C  E  V  U  S  F  E  L  J  L
V  D  X  O  G  H  C  L  W  I  R  R  N  T  L  L  D  S  F  D
E  E  F  X  G  R  D  Q  T  U  E  K  C  T  H  S  E  T  E  S
B  S  S  Q  H  V  I  N  U  S  C  N  M  A  A  I  Z  N  V  P
R  T  Z  I  E  G  A  Z  E  E  I  P  F  R  C  T  E  X  W  H
E  R  L  E  Z  L  S  R  Z  T  G  D  O  E  H  T  I  Z  B  K
E  U  G  D  T  Y  P  V  X  L  R  N  P  A  A  G  D  O  O  R
D  C  P  A  E  B  C  E  H  Q  Y  S  A  E  C  M  V  B  N  F
I  T  B  V  T  T  E  S  H  G  G  B  R  T  F  H  Z  C  D  D
N  I  L  Y  E  B  A  N  A  J  D  H  E  H  I  A  I  U  F  E
G  O  U  T  T  A  E  M  Q  T  Z  L  A  L  V  K  N  U  M
N  N  L  Y  B  D  P  B  W  G  F  O  A  T  R  L  E  N  G  L
```

Name: _____ Date: _____

Organisms in Danger

CROSSWORD PUZZLE

DIRECTIONS: Complete the crossword puzzle.

ACROSS

2. killing or removing wildlife from its habitat illegally

4. a species in danger of becoming extinct

5. a species that is close to becoming endangered

7. mating of endangered or threatened species in zoos or preserves

8. different species living in the same area

9. no living organisms of a species exist

10. an organism's natural habitat is changed by humans or nature

DOWN

1. a species that plays an important part in the lives of other species in an ecosystem

2. protecting an entire ecosystem to prevent habitat loss

3. when an organism's natural habitat is split into smaller pieces by roads that are built through an area

6. a group of organisms that have similar characteristics

Learning about Ecosystems

DIRECTIONS: Context clues help us learn new words when we read. Use the words, phrases, and sentences around new words to determine their meanings. Look at the words in the chart and fill in the column "What I Think It Means." Read the passage and look for context clues to help determine the meanings of the words. Then, fill in the last column, "What It Means in Context." If your answer in the first column was completely correct, use the second column to add something to the word's meaning beyond your original ideas.

Word	What I Think It Means	What It Means in Context
biome		
ecosystem		
ecologist		
food chain		
food webs		

Have you ever walked through a thick, plant-filled forest? Or, have you driven through a hot, sandy desert? If you have, you have been in one of Earth's many biomes. A **biome** is a large area that has the same type of climate, weather, plants, and animals. Most of Earth's biomes are on land. There are biomes that are very cold, where the plants are very small and low to the ground. Other biomes are very hot, and there are not many plants at all.

Within each biome, there may be many ecosystems. An **ecosystem** is all of the living and nonliving things in a certain area. A type of scientist called an **ecologist** studies how these things interact with each other. For example, squirrels need a safe supply of water. If squirrels cannot find enough clean drinking water, they might move to another area to find water.

In each ecosystem, there are many types organisms. All of the plants and animals in an ecosystem depend on each other. Most plants are producers. They make their own energy through photosynthesis by capturing the sun's energy. Animals are consumers. They eat plants or other animals for energy. When animals eat plants and those animals eat other animals, it is called a **food chain**. Each ecosystem has many food chains. When they overlap, they form **food webs**.

ECOSYSTEMS AND BIOMES

Pieces of the Ecosystem Puzzle

WORD SEARCH

DIRECTIONS: Find the ecosystems vocabulary words in the word search below. Words can be found down, across, and diagonally. Then, on a separate piece of paper, write sentences for five of the words.

WORD BANK

ecosystem	biotic factors	water	oxygen	population	ecology
habitat	abiotic factors	sunlight	soil	community	

```
R  Z  E  G  Y  S  A  A  P  H  I  D  N  T  N  V  N  W  E  J
V  K  M  E  L  R  M  B  X  W  F  O  H  K  S  Y  F  J  J  A
P  Y  R  L  U  O  L  I  M  M  X  E  M  A  X  Z  X  X  H  G
F  Q  S  C  Q  I  C  O  Y  G  R  Y  M  O  B  E  K  X  X  G
C  H  E  R  O  E  O  T  N  M  F  I  T  T  X  I  A  B  N  C
E  C  C  S  R  C  M  I  T  X  J  H  N  T  I  S  T  E  S  C
I  A  O  Y  B  O  M  C  R  H  L  X  I  Z  B  I  G  A  X  Z
Q  C  S  T  I  L  U  F  J  P  K  Y  L  X  M  Y  G  Q  T  P
V  G  Y  T  O  O  N  A  P  P  N  D  B  B  X  H  W  M  S  X
T  F  S  M  T  G  I  C  F  P  H  C  E  O  H  T  A  D  I  U
Q  A  T  H  I  Y  T  T  B  Y  O  U  I  X  P  E  T  I  I  U
P  B  E  J  C  M  Y  O  X  W  I  P  V  J  L  P  E  L  Z  W
I  F  M  E  F  G  C  R  J  K  G  H  U  T  O  M  R  E  H  I
O  L  Q  S  A  F  J  S  N  C  N  O  H  L  M  S  E  X  Y  Q
P  Z  Y  I  C  N  J  Z  W  F  W  G  O  T  A  W  W  P  R  Q
N  M  B  Y  T  Y  G  K  P  H  I  V  I  U  Q  T  H  V  L  D
K  P  P  I  O  X  A  H  M  L  N  N  E  I  O  B  I  P  R  O
J  L  N  I  R  X  A  J  N  J  R  X  N  F  R  R  F  O  U  O
E  M  F  J  S  M  H  U  L  N  F  Q  Q  M  T  Z  Y  D  N  O
R  W  I  E  V  F  S  H  O  C  D  D  V  U  P  F  N  U  R  I
```

Name: _____   Date: _____

Pieces of the Ecosystem Puzzle

DIRECTIONS: Complete the crossword puzzle.

ACROSS

3. the nonliving parts of an ecosystem

5. all of the living and nonliving things that are located in an area

6. an abiotic part of an ecosystem; required by plants to perform photosynthesis

8. an abiotic part of an ecosystem; this liquid is required by all living things

9. the place where an organism lives that provides it with shelter, food, and water

10. an abiotic part of an ecosystem; this gas is required by all living things

DOWN

1. the study of the interaction of living and nonliving things in the environment

2. all of the members of one type of species in a specific area

4. the living parts of an ecosystem

6. an abiotic part of an ecosystem; made of small pieces of rock, water, and decaying matter

7. all of the different populations that live in a specific area

Name: _____   Date: _____

The Chains of Life

W O R D   S E A R C H

DIRECTIONS: Find the food chain and food web vocabulary words in the word search below. Words can be found down, across, and diagonally. Then, on a separate piece of paper, write sentences for five of the words.

WORD BANK

| producer | herbivore | omnivore | decomposer | food web |
| consumer | carnivore | scavenger | food chain | energy pyramid |

```
S  I  T  N  A  C  Q  O  W  Q  C  M  D  G  I  K  G  D  Q  A
H  D  N  D  A  F  R  Q  O  T  Q  Y  T  Z  J  G  A  J  Y  X
X  Z  M  A  D  F  O  O  D  C  H  A  I  N  I  I  P  C  R  V
U  E  W  G  A  C  K  U  P  J  T  V  J  G  E  F  G  S  U  S
S  N  W  V  I  A  S  A  U  G  A  V  E  U  E  I  H  W  L  S
J  E  U  P  E  R  U  F  N  A  B  W  G  O  O  K  X  M  N  A
R  R  I  R  O  N  T  O  D  F  D  R  P  E  H  X  T  J  M  H
S  G  Z  O  X  I  S  O  Z  F  O  N  R  X  X  D  R  O  S  X
C  Y  X  D  V  V  N  D  D  Q  M  O  E  U  O  E  P  G  O  O
A  P  W  U  Y  O  L  W  D  F  V  J  G  A  M  C  R  W  L  C
V  Y  A  C  F  R  G  E  U  I  K  M  N  U  D  E  Q  F  J  T
E  R  N  E  E  E  Z  B  N  Z  W  I  S  D  E  H  V  K  U  X
N  A  Z  R  M  N  H  M  E  D  J  N  Z  B  C  E  E  W  N  U
G  M  Z  M  M  H  O  Y  Z  U  O  Y  N  D  O  R  E  Z  U  L
E  I  Q  H  G  T  B  B  H  C  I  Q  V  U  M  B  K  M  F  N
R  D  X  S  T  O  T  D  C  W  H  V  V  O  P  I  P  R  C  C
M  U  O  N  L  M  M  P  J  F  P  O  J  R  O  V  B  J  F  E
J  C  T  T  T  J  Z  K  H  R  D  I  H  B  S  O  D  Z  T  X
O  E  H  Q  Z  X  G  I  H  G  P  T  N  X  E  R  D  W  K  L
K  M  J  D  S  X  W  I  J  W  F  Y  L  X  R  E  M  A  M  C
```

Name: _____   Date: _____

The Chains of Life

CROSSWORD PUZZLE

DIRECTIONS: Complete the crossword puzzle.

ACROSS

1. an organism that breaks down dead organisms and wastes

4. an organism that cannot create its own food; it eats other organisms as a food source

5. an animal that eats the remains of dead animals

7. an organism that eats only plants

9. an organism that eats both plants and animals

10. a diagram that shows the order in which organisms are eaten by other organisms; is usually drawn in a straight line and connected by arrows

DOWN

2. a triangular diagram that shows the flow of energy from one feeding level to another

3. an organism that creates its own food through photosynthesis

6. an organism that eats only animals

8. a diagram that shows overlapping food chains

Name: _____ Date: _____

The Pyramid of Life

F I L L   I N   T H E   C H A R T

A **food energy pyramid** is another way to show the flow of energy through an ecosystem. Starting at the base of the pyramid and moving toward the top, energy is lost and the number of organisms in each population becomes smaller.

DIRECTIONS: Use the first set of words in the word bank to label the energy levels of the food pyramid. Then, write the names of the organisms from the second set of words in the correct levels of the pyramid.

WORD BANK

producers	primary consumers	secondary consumers	tertiary consumers
robin	oak tree rabbit	jaguar owl	chipmunk
deer	fox cow	wheat mouse	dandelion

Biome Characteristics

DIRECTIONS: Find the biome vocabulary words in the word search below. Words can be found down, across, and diagonally. Then, on a separate piece of paper, write sentences for five of the words.

WORD BANK

biome	understory	savannah	deciduous	tundra
tropical rain forest	desert	boreal	temperate rain forest	permafrost
canopy	grassland	temperate	coniferous	taiga

```
Q  T  E  M  P  E  R  A  T  E  R  A  I  N  F  O  R  E  S  T
Y  T  I  O  Y  M  S  N  A  C  I  X  C  I  G  H  I  Y  G  Q
R  R  Q  O  X  C  R  N  C  K  S  I  D  X  M  H  D  G  L  S
C  O  A  S  S  T  I  T  R  U  D  U  L  I  S  J  V  Q  Z  F
W  P  B  R  A  N  E  O  M  H  B  L  N  U  S  Y  Z  Y  M  M
E  I  H  F  V  C  N  M  G  C  F  O  O  E  R  N  P  G  L  Q
O  C  N  U  A  L  Z  R  P  Q  B  U  Q  O  G  O  U  R  C  W
Q  A  T  A  N  B  R  Y  I  E  D  V  X  Z  N  W  N  A  F  H
K  L  U  Q  N  L  D  A  V  I  R  S  N  A  T  Z  D  S  I  G
D  R  M  V  A  U  U  F  C  T  E  A  C  B  Q  V  E  S  P  I
E  A  H  T  H  D  W  E  U  X  D  I  T  X  P  E  R  L  L  V
Q  I  O  O  Z  I  D  C  Z  I  I  J  S  E  E  T  S  A  I  X
N  N  T  R  Q  B  A  Z  T  U  N  D  R  A  R  X  T  N  V  P
K  F  A  J  C  O  N  I  F  E  R  O  U  S  M  Q  O  D  G  Q
M  O  I  B  Z  F  V  Z  G  T  F  S  M  H  A  V  R  T  K  B
C  R  G  J  O  E  J  N  R  S  S  L  Q  O  F  O  Y  V  O  O
Q  E  A  V  U  M  Q  E  X  K  K  O  S  V  R  W  F  V  K  R
R  S  F  G  O  P  S  B  I  O  M  E  M  B  O  R  U  T  Z  E
G  T  F  V  W  E  R  W  E  P  S  S  R  M  S  J  I  S  Y  A
R  F  D  Y  D  P  C  Z  U  H  D  R  K  U  T  J  M  B  B  L
```

Biome Characteristics

DIRECTIONS: Complete the crossword puzzle.

ACROSS

2. biome with plants and grasses, but no trees; receives 25–75 cm of precipitation a year

3. type of tree that loses and regrows leaves each year

4. a group of ecosystems with similar organisms and climates

5. biome that receives 50–150 cm of precipitation a year; has many scattered shrubs, tall grasses, and small trees

7. cone-producing trees with needlelike leaves that remain green all year

8. northern biome with many coniferous trees; very cold temperatures in the winter months

10. area of the forest below the canopy, where shorter plants grow

11. forest biome with many different trees, mosses, and ferns; most trees lose and regrow their leaves each year.

DOWN

1. type of rain forest biome near the equator; receives a lot of rain; temperatures are warm all year

3. biome that receives less than 25 cm of precipitation throughout the year; has many different species of cacti and reptiles

6. frozen soil

7. area of the forest that is formed by the leaves of tall trees

9. cold, dry biome, where the soil stays frozen the entire year; very little precipitation falls

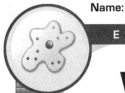

What Is Each Biome Like?

DIRECTIONS: Each **biome** has certain types of plants and animals that have adapted to living there. Use the biomes in the word bank to fill in the blank for each biome characteristic below. You will use each type of biome several times.

WORD BANK

tropical rain forest	taiga	tundra
desert	deciduous forest	grassland

1. _____ biome with the largest diversity of animal and plant life

2. _____ evergreen trees that can stand the cold temperatures

3. _____ tall canopy of trees that lets very little light through to the understory

4. _____ many types of deciduous trees, such as oaks, birches, and maples

5. _____ animals such as hawks, deer, moose, and wolves

6. _____ extreme temperatures during the day and night; very little rainfall

7. _____ large amounts of rainfall

8. _____ animals such as insects, spiders, reptiles, and birds; many inactive during the hot days

9. _____ rich soil; tall grasses that provide food and shelter for many animals

10. _____ long, cold winters

11. _____ animals such as squirrels, rabbits, wolves, and bears

12. _____ permafrost soil frozen all year long

13. _____ very few tall plants grow in the sandy or rocky soil

14. _____ conifer trees with needlelike leaves, such as pines, firs, and spruces

15. _____ thin, nutrient-poor, acidic soil

16. _____ animals such as zebras, lions, rhinoceroses, and owls

17. _____ plants such as prickly pears, yucca, and brittlebush

18. _____ animals such as polar bears, arctic foxes, and mountain goats

ECOSYSTEMS AND BIOMES

Where Are the World's Biomes?

MAP SKILLS

DIRECTIONS: Earth's **biomes** are very different from each other. They have different amounts of rainfall, kinds of climates, and types of plants and animals. Use the information from Biome Characteristics on page 111 and What Is Each Biome Like? on page 112 to help you determine where each biome is located. Use colorful pencils or crayons to color each biome on the world map below. Color the key to identify each of the major land biomes.

MAP KEY

☐ tundra ☐ taiga

☐ tropical rain forest ☐ desert

☐ grassland ☐ deciduous forest

☐ savannah

ECOSYSTEMS AND BIOMES

You Be the Ecologist

INDEPENDENT RESEARCH

DIRECTIONS: Scientists called **ecologists** spend much of their time researching biomes and the types of organisms that are found there. In this activity, you will research a biome that ecologists study. Choose one of the biomes below. Use the following questions to guide your research. Remember to use some biome vocabulary words that you have learned. If you need additional space, continue your answers on a separate piece of paper.

BIOMES

tropical rain forest	taiga	tundra
desert	deciduous forest	grassland

1. Type of biome: _____

2. Continents where this biome is located: _____

_____

3. Description of climate: _____

_____

4. Animals that are found in this biome: _____

_____

_____

5. Plants that are found in this biome: _____

_____

_____

6. Use a map to find the latitude of this biome.

   a. southernmost latitude: _____

   b. northernmost latitude: _____

7. On a separate piece of paper, draw a picture of this biome. Make sure to include animals, plants, and the climate of your chosen biome.

8. Resources: _____

_____

Name: _____   Date: _____

Biomes Throughout the Year

DIRECTIONS: The data in the chart shows the yearly temperatures of two different biomes. Create a line graph using the data from the chart. Then, answer the questions below.

Temperature (°C)		
Month	Biome 1	Biome 2
January	−10	20
February	−3	28
March	5	29
April	10	34
May	15	36
June	19	38
July	20	42
August	18	37
September	14	32
October	9	27
November	−2	25
December	−9	20

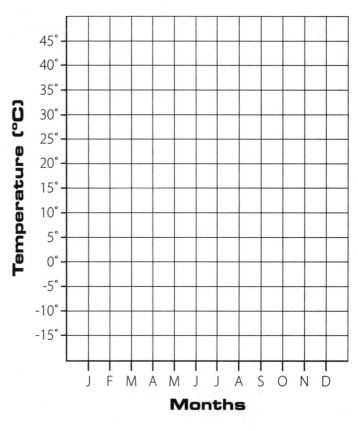

1. What is the temperature range of Biome 1? Biome 2? _____ _____

2. Based on the data and graph, describe what type of biome each set of data represents.

   _____

   _____

3. What additional data would be helpful in determining the name of each biome?

   _____

   _____

   _____

Name: _____   Date: _____

Learning about Environmental Issues

DIRECTIONS: Context clues help us learn new words when we read. Use the words, phrases, and sentences around new words to determine their meanings. Look at the words in the chart and fill in the column "What I Think It Means." Read the passage and look for context clues to help determine the meanings of the words. Then, fill in the last column, "What It Means in Context." If your answer in the first column was completely correct, use the second column to add something to the word's meaning beyond your original ideas.

Word	What I Think It Means	What It Means in Context
preserve		
pollution		
recycle		
compost		
organic		

In recent years, many people have been concerned about the health of our environment. Humans are destroying natural areas, such as forests, swamps, and grasslands, to build homes and businesses. Many people want to **preserve** these areas so that the plants and animals that live there will not be disturbed.

Without always knowing it, humans create **pollution** that can damage these natural areas. Pollution is any change that causes damage to soil, air, water, or an organism. Even something as simple as throwing a plastic bag on the ground can damage nature. The bag will be carried by runoff or blown by wind into streams or rivers and may eventually wind up in the ocean. There, it might be eaten by an animal that mistakes the bag for food. The animal might choke on this plastic bag and die.

How can you prevent the amount of pollution that you make? You can **recycle** materials that you use. For example, after you have finished using a plastic water bottle, you can recycle it. The bottle can be made into new plastic bottles or turned into thin threads and woven into carpets or clothing.

Many people **compost** organic material. Composting is when **organic** materials, such as fruit peels, vegetables, leaves, and sticks, are piled up. After a few months, with the help of bacteria, worms, and heat from the sun, these materials turn into new soil. This soil can be used as a rich fertilizer in a garden. Composting also cuts down on the amount of waste that is sent to landfills.

Name: _____   Date: _____

Environmental Issues

DIRECTIONS: Find the environmental issues vocabulary words in the word search below. Words can be found down, across, and diagonally. Then, on a separate piece of paper, write sentences for five of the words.

WORD BANK

acid rain	erosion	recycle	greenhouse effect
compost	fossil fuel	reduce	ozone layer
conservation	litter	smog	
energy	pollution	reuse	
global warming	preservation	renewable resource	

```
N  G  B  D  Z  E  G  G  C  Q  X  D  X  U  F  I  K  F  K  G
B  G  R  E  E  N  H  O  U  S  E  E  F  F  E  C  T  Z  G  P
C  B  G  J  R  R  G  X  C  B  T  M  M  O  X  P  O  B  V
L  R  X  W  Z  A  C  I  D  R  A  I  N  U  F  G  M  I  E  W
W  E  W  S  A  C  O  N  T  P  I  E  T  U  S  S  I  I  R  Z
B  N  O  Q  I  R  E  U  S  E  O  U  B  V  T  M  V  G  O  A
W  E  Z  C  E  G  P  J  C  R  Y  L  R  E  D  U  C  E  S  V
Q  W  O  B  P  L  X  R  P  O  E  A  L  B  O  K  U  I  I  Y
A  A  N  B  F  O  T  U  E  I  N  C  E  U  S  Z  T  Q  O  C
W  B  E  A  O  B  O  R  Z  S  Q  S  Y  I  T  C  J  T  N  M
F  L  L  E  S  A  Q  L  F  R  E  Y  E  C  H  I  T  Q  G  E
R  E  A  A  S  L  X  M  N  U  G  R  Y  R  L  T  O  J  S  Y
X  R  Y  S  I  W  I  C  Q  B  Y  F  V  V  E  Q  N  X  S
X  E  E  E  L  A  N  T  Y  V  D  T  J  A  O  A  W  V  O  D
H  S  R  N  F  R  R  L  T  S  K  P  B  D  T  W  T  F  N  Y
F  O  Q  E  U  M  I  E  F  E  W  F  V  L  M  I  F  I  M  G
G  U  P  R  E  I  R  K  H  C  R  R  V  F  A  J  O  I  O  E
B  R  Z  G  L  N  Z  D  P  F  E  S  C  U  Q  R  Y  N  U  N
P  C  Z  Y  H  G  X  W  M  D  L  C  P  L  D  T  S  X  Z  H
F  E  M  X  S  S  G  J  Q  G  Y  N  J  C  O  M  P  O  S  T
```

Environmental Issues

DIRECTIONS: Complete the crossword puzzle.

ACROSS

2. an Earth material or energy that can be replaced after it is used

5. trash or garbage that is scattered around

6. thick, brown haze that forms when pollution in the air reacts with sunlight

8. a toxic form of oxygen made when pollution mixes with sunlight; a major chemical in smog

9. formed from the remains of plant or animals; used to create energy

10. a theory that states that the average temperature of Earth is increasing due to the amount of carbon dioxide gas in the atmosphere

11. to turn an object into something different after using it

12. when certain gases get trapped in Earth's atmosphere and block heat from leaving, causing Earth's temperature to rise

DOWN

1. preservation or reduced use of an object, such as water, electricity, or Earth materials

3. precipitation that is changed by exhaust that is released from cars, trucks, and power plants

4. to turn organic material into soil

7. a layer of the atmosphere that protects Earth from UV rays that come from the sun

HUMANS AND THE ENVIRONMENT

Pollution Solution

INDEPENDENT RESEARCH

DIRECTIONS: Many conservationists and environmental activists are making efforts to cut down on the amount of pollution that humans create, and so can you. The following chart lists common pollution-related problems. Use science books, encyclopedias, or the Internet to research possible solutions to these problems. In the first column, list solutions that other people may have tried. In the second column, think of your own solutions.

Pollution Problem	Common Solutions	My Own Solution
Litter in a storm gutter is clogging a street sewer grate.		
Animal waste from a farm is causing bad odors at a nearby school.		
When your neighbor burns leaves in the fall, the smoke bothers your allergies.		
Old furniture and appliances are dumped along a local road.		
A paper factory releases hot water into a river, which kills wildlife.		
A local landfill is nearly full of tires, aluminum cans, and newspapers.		

Ways You Can Help the Environment

DIRECTIONS: You can help preserve the environment that you see around you. In the **cause** column of the chart below, read some of the ways that people have helped plants and animals. In the **effect** column, write ways that the causes help the local environment improve. Think of a time when you or someone you know helped the environment. Write your own cause and effect story in the last row of the chart.

Cause	Effect
Anthony and his mother were in the car. He yelled to his mother that she was about to run over a turtle. She pulled over the car and got out. She moved the turtle to the side of the road.	
Milkweed is growing in a field but will be destroyed this winter when new houses are built. In the fall, Judy and Marsha gathered some of the milkweed seeds. They got their parents' permission to plant the seeds in their backyards.	
David was rowing his canoe through the creek. He saw a large bird stuck in a net along the shore. He asked his dad to help him rescue the bird. They took the injured bird to the veterinarian. The doctor removed the bird from the net and threw the net in the trash.	

Name: _____   Date: _____

Reduce, Reuse, and Recycle

DIRECTIONS: In order to keep our environment clean and free of wastes that we create, it is important for us to use our natural resources wisely. Three simple practices that can help are reducing, reusing, and recycling. Use the charts below to brainstorm ways that you can reduce, reuse, and recycle at your home or school.

REDUCE
Cut down on the amount of a resource that we use.

Example:
Use less water by taking a shorter shower.

_____

_____

_____

_____

_____

REUSE
Use an item again.

Example:
Save cups from a fast food restaurant.

_____

_____

_____

_____

_____

RECYCLE
Change the object back into an earlier form of itself and make something new.

Example:
Recycle newspapers into writing paper.

_____

_____

_____

_____

_____

Learning about Living Things (page 9)

alive–showing aspects of life, such as growing, reproducing, and responding to stimuli

cells–the basic units of living things

develop–to grow and change

respond–to react to a stimulus

reproduce–to create a new object that is similar in appearance to the original

It's Alive! (page 10)

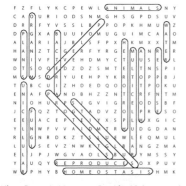

What Does It Mean to Be Alive? (page 11)

1. organism, N
2. unicellular, N
3. multicellular, T
4. autotroph, A
5. response, P
6. develop, E, O
7. reproduce, U
8. heterotroph, O
9. homeostasis, S
10. stimulus, S

Mystery Word: spontaneous

Scientists Who Study Life (page 12)

1. botanists
2. ecologists
3. marine biologists
4. cell biologists
5. microbiologists
6. geneticists
7. agronomists
8. zoologists
9. biologists
10. entomologists
11. paleontologists
12. anthropologists

Learning about Cells (page 13)

unicellular–an organism made of only one cell

multicellular–an organism made of many cells

microscope–a device for viewing tiny objects

organelles–small organs found within a cell

nucleus–the control center of a cell

function–to work; a job

The Amazing Microscope (page 14)

1. ocular (eyepiece)
2. body tube
3. arm
4. coarse focus knob
5. fine focus knob
6. base
7. nosepiece
8. objectives
9. stage clips
10. stage
11. diaphragm
12. light source

What Is Inside a Cell? (page 15)

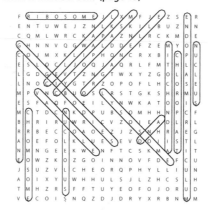

What Is Inside a Cell (page 16)

ACROSS

2. Golgi bodies
4. lysosome
7. cell wall
8. cytoplasm
10. chloroplast
12. chromosomes
13. endoplasmic reticulum

DOWN

1. ribosomes
3. organelle
5. nucleus
6. mitochondria
7. cell membrane
9. nucleolus
11. vacuole

Label an Animal Cell (page 17)

1. endoplasmic reticulum
2. nucleus
3. lysosome
4. Golgi body
5. vacuole
6. cell membrane
7. nucleolus
8. chromosomes
9. mitochondria
10. cytoplasm
11. ribosomes

Label a Plant Cell (page 18)

1. chloroplast
2. vacuole
3. mitochondrion
4. cell wall
5. cytoplasm
6. cell membrane
7. endoplasmic reticulum
8. nucleolus
9. chromosomes
10. nucleus

Comparing Plant and Animal Cells (page 19)

1. both
2. plant
3. both
4. both
5. plant
6. animal
7. plant
8. both
9. animal
10. both
11. both
12. plant

13. Answers will vary but may include sunflowers, pea plants, and apple trees.
14. Answers will vary but may include turtles, dogs, and humans.
15. Paragraphs will vary but should include similarities and differences between plant and animal cells.

Looking at Living Cells (page 21)

Drawings and observations will vary.

Can You Tell If It Is a Cell? (page 22)

1. 3, 60%
2. She found chloroplasts in the sample, so it may be a plant cell.
3. No; there are no chloroplasts.
4. It is either slide 2 or 4 because there are no cells walls or chloroplasts. There is a nucleus in each of the cells. It is most likely 4, since it is unicellular.
5. She can look at other cells taken from the same location and compare them.

The Mystery of Cells (page 23)

1. replace, C
2. nucleus, L
3. organelles, L
4. interphase, E
5. cells, C
6. identical, L
7. chromosomes, C
8. chlorophyll, Y
9. endoplasmic reticulum, E

Creating a Cell Model (page 24)

Models will vary, but materials chosen should reflect the shape or function of each organelle.

Why Do I Look Like Me? (page 27)

1. Answers will vary.
2. Tongue rolling, bent little finger, and straight thumb may be more difficult to predict because those traits are not visible all of the time.
3. Yes, if both parents pass on a recessive gene, you can display that recessive trait.

The Cell Cycle (page 28)

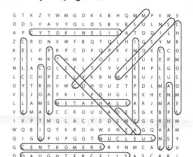

The Cell Cycle (page 29)

ACROSS

2. cell membrane
4. interphase
5. chromosomes
7. centromere
8. cytokinesis
9. DNA

DOWN

1. daughter cells
3. mitosis
5. chromatids
6. nucleus

Cellular Division (page 30)

1. 120 million
2. 7 times
3. 2,880 hours; 172,800 minutes; 10,368,000 seconds
4. 23 chromosomes
5. 2, 4, 8, 16, 32, 64, 128, 256, 512, 1,024

Learning about Classification (page 31)

organisms–living things
kingdoms–the major groups in which all living things are placed for identification
characteristics–special traits that help identify an object
species–smallest, most specific group into which an organism can be classified
vertebrate–an animal with a backbone

A System of Organization (page 32)

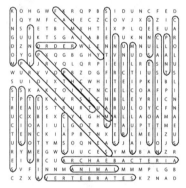

A System of Organization (page 33)

ACROSS
2. invertebrates 10. archaebacteria
3. plant 11. protist
9. fungi 12. taxonomy

DOWN
1. vertebrates 6. eukaryotes
4. animal 7. prokaryotes
5. Linnaeus 8. eubacteria

Classifying Everyday Objects (page 34)

Part 1:

backpack–pencil, notebook, textbook, paper, calculator
gym bag–tennis shoes, socks, gym shorts, deodorant, towel
purse–lipstick, key ring, cell phone, wallet, checkbook

Part 2: Answers will vary but may include:

land animals–bear, snake, tortoise, squirrel, monkey
flying animals–hawk, goose, owl, raven, mosquito
water animals–frog, alligator, whale, trout, crab

Let Me Count the Ways (page 35)

Answers will vary.

Remembering Taxonomy (page 36)

Answers will vary.

How Scientists Classify Living Things (page 37)

1. classification
2. kingdoms
3. fungi
4. plant
5. mammals
6. animal
7. vertebrates
8. invertebrates
9. species
10. nonvascular
11. amphibians
12. protists
   eubacteria
   archaebacteria

The Diversity of Life (page 38)

1. 1,400,000 species of insects
2. 160 species
3. 7,916.67 liters
4. 160 legs
5. a. 67% b. 1/3 c. 100%

Discovering New Rain Forest Species (page 39)

1. The snail may be a new species because there were 21 snails observed. This could be a colony of a new type of snail.
2. The tiger and butterfly may be rare animals within their own species. The tiger could be albino, and the butterfly could have a birth defect or may have lost its antennae to a predator.
3. The purple fern-like plant may be a new species based on the large number seen.
4. You would have to collect additional data over several days or months. If you see more examples of these new organisms, you might be able to conclude that they are new species.
5. In the rain forest, the snail might have different types of food sources than elsewhere on Earth. There may also be fewer natural predators in the area, and if the snails live longer, they could grow bigger or there may be less human interference in their environment.

The Classified Ads (page 40)

Advertisements will vary.

Comparing the Kingdoms (page 41)

1. Protist, plant-like, unicellular, autotroph
2. Plant, multicellular, autotroph
3. Fungi, multicellular, decomposer, heterotroph
4. Animal, multicellular, heterotroph
5. Eubacteria, prokaryote, unicellular
6. Animal, multicellular, heterotroph
7. Protist, plant-like, multicellular, autotroph
8. Protist, animal-like, unicellular, heterotroph
9. Fungi, unicellular, heterotroph
10. Animal, multicellular, heterotroph
11. Animal, multicellular, heterotroph
12. Plant, multicellular, autotroph
13. Animal, multicellular, heterotroph
14. Protist, fungi-like, unicellular, heterotroph
15. Animal, multicellular, heterotroph
16. Animal, multicellular, heterotroph
17. Animal, multicellular, heterotroph
18. Protist, fungi-like, unicellular, heterotroph
19. Archaebacteria, unicellular, heterotroph, live in extreme environments

Learning about Simple Life Forms (page 42)

bacteria–single-celled organisms; have no nucleus; some types are helpful, some are harmful
protist–a kingdom of diverse organisms; every protist cell has an organized nucleus
parasites–organisms that live in or on a host; often cause harm to that organism
fungi–a kingdom of multicellular, heterotrophic organisms
mold–a type of fungi that can grow on food

Simple Life Forms (page 43)

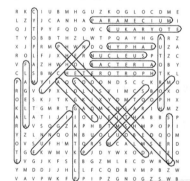

Simple Life Forms (page 44)

ACROSS
5. lichen 12. prokaryote
9. nucleus 13. autotroph
10. bacteria

DOWN
1. hyphae 6. spores
2. archaebacteria 7. eukaryote
3. heterotroph 8. flagella
4. algae 11. protist

The Eubacteria Kingdom (page 45)

1. plasma membrane
2. ribosomes
3. flagellum
4. DNA
5. cell wall
6. cytoplasm
7. disease
8. prokaryotes
9. rod, spiral, sphere
10. flagella
11. yogurt

Bacteria: Community Helper? (page 46)

1. b
2. c
3. a
4. e
5. d
6. g
7. j
8. f
9. i
10. h

The Protist Kingdom (page 47)

1. cilia
2. macronucleus
3. food vacuole
4. cytoplasm
5. anal pore
6. oral groove
7. micronucleus
8. cell membrane
9. gas bladder
10. blade
11. frond
12. stipe
13. holdfast

The Tale of Two Types of Protists (page 48)

1. cytoplasm, Y, S
2. freshwater, E, T
3. vacuole, U
4. anal pore, A, O
5. marine, M, I, E
6. holdfast, O, T
7. gas bladders, R
8. blades, S
9. giant kelp, K

Mystery Words: eukaryotes, moist

The Fungi Kingdom (page 49)

1. cap
2. gills
3. hyphae
4. scales
5. stalk
6. cap
7. gills
8. hyphae
9. stalk
10. scales

You Be the Microbiologist (page 50)

Answers will vary.

Lichens, Mosses, and Algae (page 52)

1. Answers will vary based on student observations.
2. Students should be able to observe cells in each sample. Any organism with cells is or was once alive.

Life as a One-Celled Organism (page 53)

Answers will vary.

How Well Do Household Cleaners Work? (page 54)

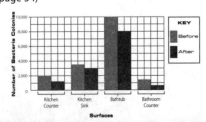

1. yes
2. 20%
3. 800 colonies
4. 4,100 colonies

5. The cleaner was most effective on the bathroom counter, because 57% of the bacteria colonies were destroyed.

Learning about the Plant Kingdom (page 55)

vascular–having a system of tubes or vessels that transport materials, such as water and nutrients

nonvascular–lacking a system of tubes or vessels

conifers–cone-producing plants

annual–a plant that completes its life cycle within a growing season

perennial–a plant that lives from year to year, producing new growth and flowers during the spring

A Kingdom of Plants (page 56)

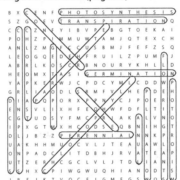

A Kingdom of Plants (page 57)

ACROSS
4. deciduous
6. chlorophyll
8. transpiration
9. germination

DOWN
1. phototropism
2. pollination
3. parachute
5. spore
6. conifer
7. geotropism

Parts of Vascular Plants (page 58)

1. flower
2. leaves
3. roots
4. seeds
5. stem
6. leaves
7. flower
8. stem
9. roots
10. seeds

Comparing Plants (page 59)

1. F, CB, FP
2. F
3. F
4. FP
5. FP
6. F
7. CB, FP
8. CB
9. CB, FP
10. CB
11. CB
12. F, CB, FP
13. F, CB, FP
14. FP
15. CB

Getting the Seeds Out (page 60)

1. water
2. birds, mammals
3. birds
4. birds, mammals
5. mammals
6. mammals
7. mammals
8. wind, water
9. mammals, water
10. wind

11. If the seeds were not dispersed, they would grow around the parent plant and compete for resources. The new plants would not grow as well.

What Is Inside a Seed? (page 61)

1. seed coat
2. embryo
3. cotyledon
4. cotyledon
5. seed coat
6. embryo
7. embryo
8. cotyledon
9. seed coat

When Seeds Fly (page 63)

1. Most plants are stationary and cannot move to deposit seeds elsewhere.
2. Plants cannot control where flying seeds will land. Some will land in areas where the conditions will not support the germination of the seed.
3. The same percentage of seeds as those in fertile areas had a chance. Without the paper, the experiment would have suggested that all seeds would germinate.
4. The fan provides a constant air speed. Outside, there might be gusts of wind or no wind at all. The experiment is predictable if repeated, but outdoors, the wind conditions may or may not support the effort of the plant to reproduce successfully.
5. Some seeds travel by wind, water, or animals.
6. More seeds increase the chances of survival because many seeds land in unfertile areas.

Growing Up, Growing Down (page 64)

Phototropism Drawings–The plant should be drawn moving toward the light in each picture.

Geotropism Drawing–The root of the plant should be drawn growing downward in the soil.

Growing Up, Growing Down (continued)

These steps would demonstrate geotropism:

1. Place some beans between two moist paper towels. Keep the towels moist and in sunlight until the beans sprout.
2. Select a seed that has a sprout that is growing straight. Pierce the seed with a long pin or needle. Stick this pin into the narrower end of a cork.
3. Place a damp paper towel into a bottle.
4. Place the seedling in the bottle and close the bottle with the cork. Place the bottle in a dark place. Observe the bottle every hour.
5. Turn the bottle every day to see the roots' response to gravity.

You Be the Botanist (page 65)

Answers will vary.

Year After Year (page 66)

1. producers, P, S
2. evergreen, E
3. roots, R
4. annual, N
5. seed, E
6. nonvascular, N, A
7. needles, L
8. niche, I

Mystery word: perennials

Plant Reproduction (page 67)

1. 3 packages will grow 27 plants.
2. 4 plants
3. 3 stalks
4. 140 plants
5. 12 miles (19.3 km)
6. 8 plants

Graphing Plant Growth (page 68)

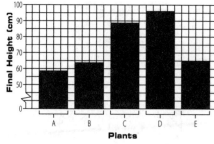

Part 1:
1. 74.4 cm
2. 38 cm
3. Plant D may have received more sunlight or water. Plant A might have a disease or may have been eaten by animals while it was growing.

Part 2:

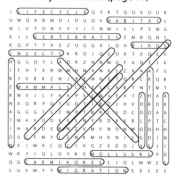

4. 18 cm
5. about 38 cm
6. about 55 cm

Learning about the Animal Kingdom (page 70)

1. heterotrophs–organisms that cannot make their own food, and they eat other organisms for energy
2. tissues–groups of similar cells that work together to do certain jobs
3. invertebrates–animals that do not have backbones
4. carnivores–organisms that eat only animals as a food source
5. omnivores–organisms that eat both plants and animals

The Diversity of Animals (page 71)

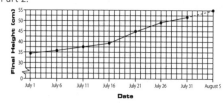

So Many Different Animals (page 72)

1. mollusks
2. amphibians
3. arachnids
4. arthropods
5. birds
6. crustaceans
7. mammals
8. fish
9. reptiles
10. zoology
11. insects
12. hibernation

Organization of Organisms (page 73)

1. a
2. d
3. b
4. c
5. An amoeba has only one cell; it is a single-celled organism. It does not combine with other amoebas to make tissues or organs.
6. A flower has cells, tissues, and organs. The tissues combine to make organs. These organs help the flower transport nutrients and water and aid in reproduction.
7. A cat has cells, tissues, and organs. The organs of the cat work together to help the cat perform life functions, such as breathing, eating, and moving. The organs form organ systems.
8. A heart has cells and tissues. It is an organ. The heart works as part of the circulatory system, which delivers oxygen and nutrients to the organism's cells.

Observing Animal Objects (page 74)

Answers will vary.

Life Cycle of a Frog (page 76)

1. spawn (egg mass)
2. embryo
3. tadpole with hind legs
4. tadpole with hind legs and forelegs
5. froglet
6. frog

The correct sequence of events is 5,4,2,6,3,1

Life Cycle of a Butterfly (page 77)

1. egg
2. caterpillar
3. chrysalis
4. butterfly

The correct sequence of events is 4,2,1,3

Vertebrate Animals (page 78)

1. moray eel
2. bullfrog
3. tiger salamander
4. chameleon
5. rattlesnake
6. hummingbird

Invertebrate Animals (page 79)

1. sponge
2. jellyfish
3. coral
4. snail
5. clam
6. roundworm
7. octopus
8. crawfish
9. spider
10. butterfly
11. starfish
12. sea urchin

What Animals Need to Survive (page 81)

1. box turtle
   food: plants
   water source: ponds or streams
   shelter: burrows or under fallen trees
2. cardinal
   food: fruits and seeds
   water source: creeks or ponds
   shelter: in a brushy woodland
3. bullfrog
   food: insects, fish, and small mammals
   water source: ponds or lakes
   shelter: burrows
4. goose
   food: plants
   water source: ponds or lakes
   shelter: nests close to water
5. squirrel
   food: acorns
   water source: streams or creeks
   shelter: nests high in trees
6.–10. Answers will vary.

You Be the Zoologist (page 82)

Answers will vary.

Amazing Animal Facts (page 83)

1. 216 eggs
2. 12 eggs
3. 6,400 eggs
4. 36,000 gallons
5. 50,400 mosquitoes
6. 16 cells
7. about 18 times
8. 1,120 lb.

Snakes in the Desert (page 84)

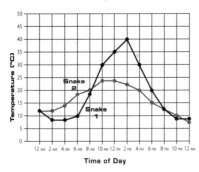

1. A snake's temperature changes throughout the day because it is a cold-blooded animal. Its body temperature is dependent on the temperature of its environment.
2. Snake 1 was exposed to the sun's rays for most of the day. Its body temperature was high around the middle of the day, when it would have been the hottest. Snake 2 stayed around the same temperature throughout the day. It was probably in a shady area or hiding between the cracks in some rocks.

Learning about the Human Body (page 85)

organs–groups of tissues that combine to perform a specific job
circulatory–the system of organs that carries blood throughout the body
respiratory–the system of organs that takes oxygen into the body and releases carbon dioxide
digestive–the system of organs that breaks down food into nutrients that the body can use
esophagus–a muscular organ that carries food from the mouth to the stomach
muscles–organs that enable the body to move

Human Body Organs and Systems (page 86)

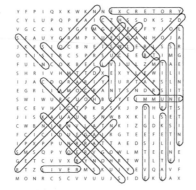

Organ Systems of the Human Body (page 87)

1. h
2. a
3. f
4. c
5. e
6. g
7. d
8. i
9. b

Magic Number: 15

Name That Body System (page 88)

1. circulatory
2. digestive
3. skeletal
4. muscular
5. respiratory
6. nervous

Human Organs and Organ Systems (page 89)

Skeletal—S
Digestive—D
Muscular—M
Nervous—N
Immune—I
Respiratory—R
Circulatory—C
Excretory—E

skull—S, D, M, N
femur—S, M, I, C
vertebrae—S, M, N
stomach—D, M, I
intestines—D, M, C
mouth—D, M, I, R
esophagus—D, M
kidneys—C, E
eyes—M, N
brain—S, D, M, N, I, R, C, E
spinal cord—S, D, M, N, I, R, C, E
nose—I, R, E
skin—N, I, E
lungs—M, R, C, E
trachea—R, E
epiglottis—D, R, E
heart—M, N, R, C, E
arteries—S, D, M, N, I, R, C
capillaries—S, D, M, N, I, R, C, E
veins—S, D, M, N, I, R, C, E

How Does Exercise Affect Your Heart Rate? (page 90)

Answers will vary.

Amazing Human Body Math Facts (page 91)

1. 360,000,000 neurons
2. 5%
3. about 17,000 a day, about 1,063 times an hour, about 18 times a minute
4. 54,000,000,000 blood cells
5. 120 pounds
6. 8,395,000 times, 167,900,000 times, 410,750,000 times

Digestion Math (page 92)

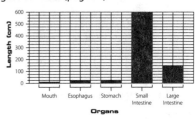

1. 807.5 cm
2. 74%
3. 19%
4. 4 times longer

A Day in the Life of a Cell (page 93)

Answers will vary.

Learning about Adaptations (page 94)

diversity–a variety of objects
adaptations–physical structures on organisms that help them survive in their environment
marine–ocean environment
finches–a type of bird that Darwin studied on the Galapagos Islands
theory–an idea that is based on observations and collected data

Changes Over Time (page 95)

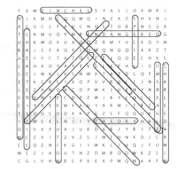

Changes Over Time (page 96)

ACROSS
1. natural selection
4. variations
6. camouflage
8. tortoises
10. structure
11. finches

DOWN
2. adaptation
3. species
5. evolution
7. theory
9. Darwin

Name the Animal Adaptation (page 97)

1. hedgehog, H
2. camel, A
3. koala, O, A
4. sea otter, S, T
5. python, N
6. bullfrog, R, O
7. beaver, V
8. wallaroo, A
9. giraffe, I
10. squirrel monkey, M, N
11. red panda, N

Mystery Words: Savannah Monitor

More Than One Way to Hide (page 98)

1. disguise
2. patterns
3. mimicry
4. blending
5. patterns
6. disguise
7. mimicry
8. mimicry
9. blending
10. counter shading
11. mimicry
12. blending
13. mimicry
14. blending
15. counter shading

Plant Adaptations (page 99)

1. b
2. d
3. a
4. c
5. g
6. e
7. f
8. i
9. h
10. j

Bird Adaptations (page 100)

3. Descriptions of birds will vary but should be appropriate for the type of habitat in which the bird would be found.
4. Changes in adaptations will vary. Students should understand that the bird species would need to adapt or the species would not survive.

Creating New Adaptations (page 101)

Answers will vary.

Organisms in Danger (page 102)

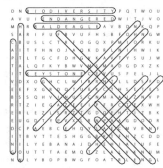

Organisms in Danger (page 103)

ACROSS
2. poaching
4. endangered
5. threatened
7. captive breeding
8. biodiversity
9. extinct
10. habitat destruction

DOWN
1. keystone
2. preservation
3. fragmentation
6. species

Learning about Ecosystems (page 104)

biome–a large area that has the same type of climate, weather, plants, and animals

ecosystem–all of the living and nonliving things in an area

ecologist–a type of scientist who studies how living and nonliving things interact in an ecosystem

food chain–the order of food consumption in an ecosystem, with producers getting energy from the sun and consumers eating producers.

food webs–several interwoven and dependent food chains

Pieces of the Ecosystem Puzzle (page 105)

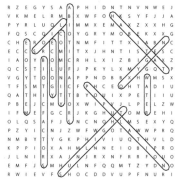

Pieces of the Ecosystem Puzzle (page 106)

ACROSS
3. abiotic factors
5. ecosystem
6. sunlight
8. water
9. habitat
10. oxygen

DOWN
1. ecology
2. population
4. biotic factors
6. soil
7. community

The Chains of Life (page 107)

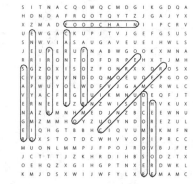

The Chains of Life (page 108)

ACROSS
1. decomposer
4. consumer
5. scavenger
7. herbivore
9. omnivore
10. food chain

DOWN
2. energy pyramid
3. producer
6. carnivore
8. food web

The Pyramid of Life (page 109)

bottom level–producers, wheat; oak tree, dandelion

second level–primary consumers; deer, rabbit, cow, mouse, chipmunk

third level–secondary consumers; owl, fox

top level–tertiary consumers; jaguar, robin

Biome Characteristics (page 110)

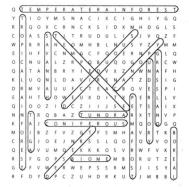

Biome Characteristics (page 111)

ACROSS
2. grassland
3. deciduous
4. biome
5. savannah
7. coniferous
8. taiga
10. understory
11. temperate

DOWN
1. tropical
3. desert
6. permafrost
7. canopy
9. tundra

What Is Each Biome Like? (page 112)

1. tropical rain forest
2. taiga
3. tropical rain forest
4 temperate forest
5. taiga
6. desert
7. tropical rain forest
8. desert
9. grassland
10. tundra
11. temperate forest
12. tundra
13. desert
14. taiga
15. taiga
16. grassland
17. desert
18. tundra

Where Are the World's Biomes? (page 113)

■ Tundra　　■ Deciduous Forest　■ Tropical Rain
■ Tiaga　　　▥ Desert　　　　　　Forest
■ Grassland　■ Savannah

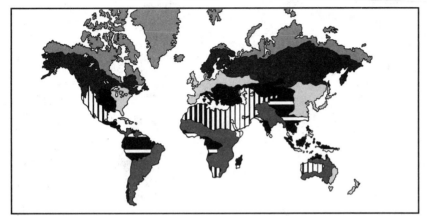

You Be the Ecologist (page 114)

Answers will vary.

Biomes Throughout the Year (page 115)

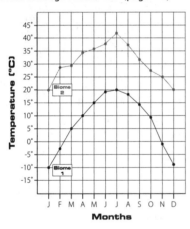

1. Biome 1: 30°C
   Biome 2: 22°C
2. Biome 1: taiga
   Biome 2: desert
3. types of plants and animals found in
   each biome, amount of precipitation

Learning about Environmental Issues (page 116)

preserve–to save or protect an object or
area for later use

pollution–waste created by humans
that can damage the environment or
other organisms

recycle–to change an object so that it can
be used again

compost–to turn organic materials into soil

organic–materials made of plant or
animal matter

Environmental Issues (page 117)

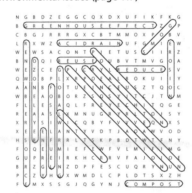

Environmental Issues (page 118)

ACROSS
2. renewable resource　9. fossil fuel
5. litter　　　　　　　　10. global warming
6. smog　　　　　　　　11. recycle
8. ozone　　　　　　　　12. greenhouse effect
DOWN
1. conservation　　　　4. compost
3. acid rain　　　　　　7. ozone layer

Pollution Solution (page 119)

Answers will vary.

Ways You Can Help the Environment (page 120)

Answers will vary, but may include:
1. The turtle could live to mate
   and reproduce.
2. The monarch butterflies will still
   have a location to lay their eggs. The
   caterpillars will still have plants to eat
   before they pupate.
3. The bird's life could be saved, and no
   other animals will get caught in the net.

Reduce, Reuse, and Recycle (page 121)

Answers will vary.